A complete guide to Adult Attention Deficit Hyperactivity Disorder (Adult ADHD)

Dr S K MUTHALIF FRCPsych (UK)

INDIA • SINGAPORE • MALAYSIA

Dedication

This book is dedicated to the countless individuals living with Adult ADHD who demonstrate remarkable resilience, perseverance, and creativity in the face of significant challenges. Their unwavering spirits, coupled with their persistent quest for self-understanding and improved wellbeing, inspire us all. It is also dedicated to the compassionate healthcare professionals – psychiatrists, psychologists, neurologists, and others – who dedicate their lives to understanding, supporting, and treating individuals with this complex condition. Your unwavering commitment to evidence-based care and your empathy for your patients are invaluable contributions to improving lives and reducing the stigma surrounding ADHD. This work is a testament to your tireless efforts, and an attempt to provide you with updated knowledge and accessible support strategies. Finally, this book is dedicated to the families and loved ones of those affected by ADHD. Your patience, understanding, and unwavering support are integral to the well-being and success of individuals navigating the complexities of this condition. Your strength and resilience deserve recognition and appreciation. The understanding and management of Adult ADHD is a collective journey, one that requires collaborative efforts, compassion, and a tireless pursuit of innovative and effective strategies.

Contents

Attention Deficit Hyperactivity Disorder (ADHD) is a condition that affects millions of individuals worldwide, impacting their daily lives and overall well-being. Dr. Shafy K Muthalif, an excellent teacher, eloquent and inspiring litterateur, and inquisitive and brilliant psychiatrist, has penned down this paradigmatic work on ADHD. With 25 years of experience in clinical psychiatry and more than a decade of exemplary clinical work within the domain of ADHD, Dr. Muthalif brings a wealth of knowledge to this important condition.

This textbook touches on imperative aspects of ADHD, including diagnosis, comorbidity, and treatment. It covers psychopharmacological, psychological, and social approaches, teaching us a holistic and biopsychosocial approach to ADHD. Dr. Muthalif's expertise as a postgraduate tutor within the NHS further enriches the content, providing readers with a comprehensive understanding of ADHD.

This work is not only a valuable resource for professionals in the field but also for anyone seeking to understand ADHD better. It is a testament to Dr. Muthalif's dedication and passion for improving the lives of those affected by ADHD.

Foreword by Dr Nismen Lathif
Consultant Psychiatrist
Post Graduate Tutor and SAS lead
Mersey care NHS Trust
United Kingdom

Preface

Adult ADHD remains significantly under-recognized and undertreated, resulting in substantial personal and societal costs. This book aims to bridge this gap by providing a comprehensive, accessible, and evidence-based resource for both individuals with ADHD and the healthcare professionals who support them. Written with a dual audience in mind – those seeking self-understanding and healthcare providers seeking the latest clinical guidance – this work integrates theoretical knowledge with practical applications. We delve into the historical context of ADHD, meticulously outlining the DSM-5 diagnostic criteria, and providing a detailed explanation of the DIVA model, a framework that effectively captures the multifaceted nature of this condition. The book offers detailed exploration of the core symptoms of Adult ADHD, moving beyond simple descriptions to provide actionable strategies for managing challenges in daily life, relationships, and the workplace. We examine both pharmacological and non-pharmacological interventions, offering a holistic approach that addresses the diverse needs of individuals with ADHD. Furthermore, the book systematically addresses common comorbidities, including anxiety, depression, and substance use disorders, providing integrated treatment approaches. Finally, it examines the latest research and future directions in Adult ADHD treatment, offering a perspective on the ongoing evolution of understanding and management of this significant condition. Our hope is that this book will empower individuals with ADHD to better understand and manage their condition, while providing healthcare professionals with up-to-date information and evidence based strategies to effectively support their patients.

1

Introduction

Adult Attention-Deficit/Hyperactivity Disorder (ADHD) is a neurodevelopmental condition that significantly impacts various aspects of an individual's life. While often diagnosed in childhood, ADHD frequently persists into adulthood, presenting unique challenges and requiring specialized treatment approaches. This book offers a comprehensive exploration of Adult ADHD, designed to be accessible and informative for both individuals living with the condition and healthcare professionals involved in its diagnosis and management. We will navigate the historical context of ADHD, highlighting the evolution of its understanding and the ongoing debates surrounding its diagnosis and prevalence. A thorough examination of the DSM-5 diagnostic criteria will be provided, emphasizing the nuances of symptom presentation in adults and the crucial importance of differentiating ADHD from other conditions sharing similar symptoms. A key feature of this book is the detailed explanation of the DIVA questionnaire for ADHD, a multifaceted framework that provides a comprehensive understanding of the condition's complexities. The DIVA model will serve as a unifying thread throughout the book, informing our discussions of symptoms, treatment options, and management strategies. We will then delve into the core symptoms of Adult ADHD – inattention, hyperactivity, impulsivity, and emotional dysregulation – exploring their manifestations in adults and presenting effective strategies for managing them. This includes practical tips for improving focus, organization, time management, and interpersonal relationships. The book also provides a comprehensive review of pharmacological and nonpharmacological interventions, including stimulant and nonstimulant medications, behavioral therapies, lifestyle modifications, and mindfulness techniques. The complexities of comorbid conditions frequently associated with Adult ADHD, such as anxiety, depression, and substance use disorders, will be addressed, providing integrated treatment approaches tailored to the individual's specific needs. Finally, we will explore the latest research and future directions in Adult ADHD treatment, encompassing emerging pharmacological approaches, innovative nonpharmacological interventions, and the exciting possibilities of personalized medicine. This book aims to equip both individuals with ADHD and healthcare professionals with the knowledge and tools necessary to effectively navigate the complexities of this condition and enhance quality of life.

2

A Historical Perspective on ADHD

The understanding of what we now know as Attention Deficit/Hyperactivity Disorder (ADHD) has undergone a dramatic transformation throughout history. Early descriptions, often shrouded in subjective interpretations and lacking the rigorous diagnostic criteria of today, paint a picture far removed from contemporary understanding. While the core symptoms – inattention, hyperactivity, and impulsivity – have been recognized across different eras and cultures, their conceptualization and treatment have evolved significantly, reflecting advancements in neuroscience, psychology, and medical practice.

One of the earliest documented accounts that bears resemblance to ADHD can be traced back to the late 19th century. While not explicitly labeled as such, various physicians described children exhibiting symptoms consistent with the disorder. These descriptions often emphasized behavioral difficulties, distractibility, and restlessness, traits that interfered with academic performance and social integration. However, the lack of standardized diagnostic tools and a unified understanding resulted in inconsistent diagnoses and varied treatment approaches. These early accounts often attributed the symptoms to moral failings, poor parenting, or even neurological damage, highlighting the limited understanding of the underlying neurobiological mechanisms.

The mid-20th century witnessed a shift in perspective. Researchers began to explore the possibility of a distinct neurological basis for these behavioral patterns. This period saw the emergence of terms like "minimal brain dysfunction" and "hyperkinetic syndrome," representing attempts to categorize these conditions more scientifically. However, these terms were often vaguely defined, leading to continued debate about the nature and etiology of the condition. The lack of consensus hampered the development of effective and consistent treatment strategies.

The landmark shift in understanding ADHD came with the publication of the Diagnostic and Statistical Manual of

Mental Disorders (DSM) in its various iterations. The DSM III, published in 1980, marked a significant milestone, introducing the term "Attention-Deficit Disorder with Hyperactivity" (ADD with H) and providing more specific diagnostic criteria. This was a pivotal moment as it provided a standardized framework for identifying and diagnosing the disorder, leading to improved consistency in clinical practice. The criteria focused on observable behaviors, making it more accessible for clinicians to diagnose.

However, even with the DSM-III introduction of clearer criteria, controversies remained. One major area of debate centered around the prevalence of

ADHD. Some argued that the diagnostic criteria were too broad, leading to overdiagnosis and inappropriate labeling of children with normal variations in behavior. Conversely, others felt the criteria were too narrow, potentially overlooking individuals who genuinely experienced the challenges associated with ADHD. This debate continues to some extent even today.

The introduction of the DSM-IV in 1994, and subsequently DSM-5 in 2013, further refined the diagnostic criteria, incorporating a more nuanced understanding of symptom presentation across different age groups and genders. The DSM-5 also distinguished between three subtypes: predominantly inattentive presentation, predominantly hyperactive-impulsive presentation, and combined presentation. This move attempted to better capture the diverse ways ADHD manifests in individuals.

Another crucial area of contention has been the biological basis of ADHD. While significant advancements in neuroscience have identified structural and functional differences in the brains of individuals with ADHD, the exact mechanisms underlying the disorder remain incompletely understood. This lack of complete biological understanding has contributed to the skepticism and controversies surrounding ADHD diagnosis and treatment, particularly regarding pharmacological interventions. Some critics have argued that the reliance on medication overemphasizes a biological model at the expense of considering psychosocial factors, creating a potential for misdiagnosis and inappropriate treatment.

Further complicating matters is the issue of comorbidity. ADHD frequently co-occurs with other conditions, such as anxiety disorders, depression, oppositional defiant disorder (ODD), and conduct disorder. These co-occurring conditions can significantly impact symptom presentation and treatment responses. Diagnosing and treating these comorbidities requires careful assessment and integrated treatment approaches. The challenge lies in distinguishing symptoms specific to ADHD from those associated with co-occurring conditions. This often necessitates collaboration between mental health professionals with diverse expertise.

The gendered nature of ADHD diagnosis also adds complexity. Historically, ADHD was largely perceived as a predominantly male disorder. Research increasingly suggests that the presentation of ADHD in girls and women may differ significantly from that in boys and men. Girls and women may exhibit more inattentive symptoms and fewer hyperactive-impulsive symptoms, potentially leading to underdiagnosis. This bias in diagnostic criteria and symptom perception has contributed to a significant gap in the identification and treatment of ADHD in females.

Moreover, cultural factors also influence the understanding and diagnosis of ADHD. What might be considered acceptable behavioral variations in one culture might be perceived as symptomatic in another. This cultural context necessitates careful consideration of cultural norms and values when assessing for ADHD. Clinicians must be aware of potential biases in their assessments and strive for culturally sensitive diagnostic practices. This awareness is crucial for accurate diagnoses and culturally appropriate treatment planning.

The evolution of our understanding of ADHD hasn't simply involved refinement of diagnostic criteria. Treatment approaches have also evolved substantially. Early interventions often focused on behavioral management techniques, such as parental training and classroom modifications. The introduction of stimulant medications in the late 20th century revolutionized treatment options, providing effective relief for many individuals experiencing significant impairment due to ADHD symptoms. However, this too has been a source of controversy. Concerns about long-term effects of medication, potential for abuse, and the overreliance on medication as a primary treatment strategy remain areas of ongoing discussion and debate.

The current landscape of ADHD research is characterized by a move towards more holistic and individualized treatment approaches. Researchers are investigating the effectiveness of non-pharmacological interventions, including cognitive behavioral therapy (CBT), mindfulness-based interventions, and neurofeedback. There is a growing emphasis on personalized medicine, tailoring interventions to meet the specific needs of individual patients, considering not only their symptom profile, but also their genetic predisposition, comorbid conditions, and psychosocial factors. This integrated approach aims to address the multifaceted nature of ADHD, moving beyond simplistic categorizations and providing more comprehensive and effective treatment. The future of ADHD research promises a deeper understanding of the underlying neurobiological mechanisms, further refinements of diagnostic criteria, and more effective and personalized treatment strategies, aiming to improve the lives of individuals affected by this complex condition. The journey of understanding ADHD is ongoing, a continuous evolution shaped by scientific advancements, evolving clinical perspectives, and the ongoing need for culturally sensitive and ethically sound treatment practices.

References

Jonkman, L. (2005). Selective attentional deficits in Children with ADHD: A review of behavioural and electrophysiological studies. https://doi.org/10.1385/1-59259-891-9:255

McCrimmon, A., Hendrickson, N., Gray, S., & Pepperdine, C. (2019). Diagnostic Frameworks in Current Canadian Educational Systems. Canadian Psychology, 60(3), 141-147.

3

DSM Diagnostic Criteria for Adult ADHD

The shift from historical interpretations to the current, more nuanced understanding of ADHD necessitates a thorough examination of the diagnostic criteria. The Diagnostic and Statistical Manual of Mental Disorders, 5th Edition (DSM-5), provides the standardized framework for diagnosing ADHD in adults. Unlike earlier diagnostic manuals, the DSM-5 emphasizes a more comprehensive and multifaceted approach, acknowledging the heterogeneity of ADHD presentations. This means that while the core symptoms remain consistent – inattention, hyperactivity, and impulsivity – their manifestation can vary significantly between individuals, leading to different subtypes and levels of severity.

The DSM-5 criteria for ADHD in adults require the presence of at least five or more symptoms of inattention or hyperactivity-impulsivity that have persisted for at least six months to a degree that is inconsistent with developmental level and negatively impacts social, academic, or occupational functioning. Crucially, several symptoms must have been present before the age of 12, although the precise age of onset may be difficult to ascertain retrospectively in adult evaluations. This retrospective element frequently relies on collateral information from family members or close friends who can provide valuable insights into the individual's developmental history.

Let's delve into the specific symptoms categorized under inattention and hyperactivity-impulsivity. Inattention symptoms include:

Often fails to give close attention to details or makes careless mistakes in schoolwork, at work, or during other activities: This isn't simply about occasional lapses in concentration; it's about a persistent pattern of inattention leading to significant errors or incomplete tasks. For example, an adult with ADHD might repeatedly overlook important details in a report, leading to errors or missed deadlines, despite understanding the consequences.

Often has difficulty sustaining attention in tasks or play activities: Maintaining focus on a single task, even one that is enjoyable, can be a significant challenge. This might manifest as frequent task-switching, difficulty completing projects, or a constant need for external stimulation to maintain engagement. For instance, an individual may start a project with enthusiasm, but their attention quickly wanders to other, less relevant tasks, resulting in incomplete or poorly executed work.

Often does not seem to listen when spoken to directly: This isn't about intentional disregard; rather, it reflects a difficulty filtering out distractions and focusing on the speaker. This can lead to misunderstandings and communication difficulties in both personal and professional settings. A common example is an adult struggling to follow a conversation, missing key pieces of information or appearing disengaged, even if they want to participate actively.

Often does not follow through on instructions and fails to finish schoolwork, chores, or duties in the workplace (not due to oppositional behavior or a failure to understand instructions): This speaks to the difficulty with task initiation and completion, often stemming from issues with planning, organization, and working memory. The individual may understand the instructions perfectly, yet fail to initiate the task or follow through to completion. For instance, an individual may consistently fail to submit assignments on time, despite acknowledging deadlines and possessing the necessary skills to complete the task.

Often has difficulty organizing tasks and activities: This can range from struggling to manage paperwork and emails to difficulty prioritizing tasks and managing time effectively. This might manifest as a disorganized workspace, missed appointments, or a general feeling of being overwhelmed by even simple tasks. Imagine an adult with a perpetually cluttered desk, perpetually missing deadlines despite setting reminders, or struggling to prioritize urgent tasks from less pressing ones.

Often avoids, dislikes, or is reluctant to engage in tasks that require sustained mental effort (such as schoolwork or homework): Procrastination is a common symptom, and it's not simply laziness. It's often a result of anticipating the difficulty of sustained focus and the potential for frustration or failure. For example, an individual may put off completing a challenging project, even when fully aware of its importance, leading to heightened stress and potential negative consequences.

Often loses things necessary for tasks or activities (e.g., school materials, pencils, books, tools, wallets, keys, paperwork, eyeglasses): This goes beyond occasional forgetfulness; it's a consistent pattern of losing essential items, often leading to frustration and inconvenience. This could include losing car keys repeatedly, misplacing important documents, or forgetting appointments because of misplaced reminders.

Often is easily distracted by extraneous stimuli:

Individuals with ADHD may struggle to filter out irrelevant information, making it difficult to concentrate on the task at hand. This could manifest as being easily distracted by noises, visual stimuli, or even internal thoughts. For example, while attempting to concentrate on reading a book, an individual may become easily distracted by a conversation in the background, a TV show playing in the next room, or even a passing thought.

Often forgetful in daily activities: This isn't just about memory lapses; it's a pattern of forgetfulness that impacts daily functioning. This might include forgetting appointments, errands, or responsibilities, even when reminders are in place. Imagine an adult repeatedly forgetting to pick up children from school, paying bills on time, or attending crucial meetings despite having set reminders.

The DSM-5 also lists hyperactivity-impulsivity symptoms:

Often fidgets with or taps hands or feet or squirms in seat: This manifests as restlessness and an inability to stay still, often leading to discomfort for both the individual and those around them. This could be seen as constant tapping, leg shaking, or restlessness even while sitting down.

Often leaves a seat in situations where remaining seated is expected: This goes beyond occasional restlessness; it's a pattern of leaving one's seat inappropriately, interrupting meetings, or disrupting activities. For example, an adult may get up repeatedly during a meeting, interrupting the speaker or causing a distraction for others.

Often runs about or climbs excessively in situations where it is inappropriate (in adolescents or adults, may be limited to feeling restless): While excessive running or climbing may be less common in adults, the underlying restlessness and difficulty staying still remain prevalent. This could manifest as pacing while talking, an inability to sit still during presentations, or a constant feeling of needing to be on the move.

Often talks excessively: This isn't simply sociability; it's an excessive amount of talking, often interrupting others or dominating conversations. It can strain relationships and lead to social difficulties. For instance, an adult might constantly interrupt conversations, dominate discussions, or talk incessantly, even when it's inappropriate or unwanted by others.

Often blurts out an answer before a question has been completed: This reflects impulsivity and a difficulty waiting for their turn to speak, frequently leading to interruptions and misunderstandings. An adult might jump in to answer a question before it's fully formulated, demonstrating a lack of patience or consideration for others' communication processes.

Often has difficulty waiting their turn (e.g., while waiting in line): This again highlights impulsivity and a difficulty with self-regulation. It can lead to frustration for both the individual and those around them. This could be seen as an adult constantly cutting lines, interrupting queues, or having difficulties waiting for their turn in any social setting.

Often interrupts or intrudes on others (e.g., butts into conversations or games): This is a demonstration of impulsivity, lacking the ability to appropriately gauge social cues and respect personal space. An adult might constantly interrupt conversations, barge into private discussions, or disregard boundaries set by others.

It's crucial to emphasize that a diagnosis of ADHD is not made solely on the basis of these symptoms. The DSM-5 criteria explicitly state that these symptoms must significantly impair social, academic, or occupational functioning. The clinician must carefully assess the individual's overall functioning to determine the level of impairment. Furthermore, it is essential to rule out other conditions that may share similar symptoms, such as anxiety disorders, bipolar disorder, and oppositional defiant disorder. A comprehensive clinical evaluation, including a thorough history, symptom assessment, and possibly neuropsychological testing, is crucial for an accurate diagnosis.

The presentation of ADHD symptoms can vary considerably across genders and cultures. Traditional diagnostic criteria might have been biased towards identifying hyperactive impulsive presentations, potentially leading to underdiagnosis of inattentive presentations, particularly in females. Similarly, cultural norms and expectations can significantly influence the expression and interpretation of ADHD symptoms. Clinicians need to be sensitive to these factors and tailor their assessment accordingly, utilizing culturally competent approaches and considering the impact of societal influences on symptom expression. A culturally informed assessment involves understanding how cultural norms might shape the manifestation of ADHD symptoms. For instance, in some cultures, hyperactivity might be considered acceptable or even encouraged in certain contexts, while in others, it might be viewed more negatively.

The diagnostic process for ADHD in adults is multifaceted, requiring careful consideration of both the DSM-5 criteria and the individual's unique circumstances. It's not just about ticking boxes; it's about understanding the individual's lived experience and how their symptoms impact their daily life. This understanding forms the crucial foundation for developing a comprehensive and individualized treatment plan. The subsequent chapters will explore the various treatment options available, emphasizing the importance of a holistic approach that combines pharmacological and nonpharmacological interventions.

References

Diagnostic And Statistical Manual Of Mental Disorders https://chitownfitness.com/stove-hill/diagnostic-and-statistical-manual-of-mental-disorders

Flisher, A. J., Sorsdahl, K., Hatherill, S., & Chehil, S. (2010). Packages of Care for Attention-Deficit Hyperactivity Disorder in Low- and Middle-Income Countries. PLOS Medicine. https://doi.org/10.1371/journal.pmed.1000235

Attention-Deficit Hyperactivity Disorder ADHD. https://www.michiganpsychologists.com/mental-health-disorders/adhd/

Martel, M. M., Levinson, C. A., Langer, J. K., & Nigg, J. T. (2016). A Network Analysis of Developmental Change in ADHD Symptom Structure from Preschool to Adulthood. https://doi.org/10.1177/2167702615618664

Weinberg, W. A., Harper, C. R., Schraufnagel, C. D., & Brumback, R. A. (1997). Attention deficit hyperactivity disorder: A disease or a symptom complex? The Journal of Pediatrics. https://doi.org/10.1016/s0022-3476(97)70257-9

Are there different types of adhd. https://thewrightinitiative.com/misc/are-there-different-types-of-adhd.html

Signs and Symptoms of ADHD. https://www.mylifenwellness.com/post/signs-and-symptoms-of-adhd

ADHD - The Practical Side - LifeEnhancementCS.com. https://lifeenhancementcs.com/blog/adhd-the-practical-side/

(1994). A focus on attention deficits. https://core.ac.uk/download/146522346.pdf

The Hidden Dangers of Substance Abuse: Understanding the Long-Term Effects on Mental Health. https://www.thenewhopemhcs.com/the-hidden-dangers-of-substance-abuse-understanding-the-long-term-effects-on-mental-health/

Weinberg, W. A., Harper, C. R., Schraufnagel, C. D., & Brumback, R. A. (1997). Attention deficit hyperactivity disorder: A disease or a symptom complex? The Journal of Pediatrics. https://doi.org/10.1016/s0022-3476(97)70257-9

4

Introducing the DIVA Model of ADHD

Building upon the established diagnostic framework of the DSM-5, understanding the complexities of adult ADHD necessitates a model that moves beyond simple symptom categorization. This is where the DIVA model proves invaluable. The DIVA model, an acronym for Deficit in Internalizing, Vigilance, and Attention, offers a compelling framework for understanding the neurocognitive underpinnings of ADHD, moving beyond the traditional focus on just inattention, hyperactivity, and impulsivity. It posits that the core deficit in ADHD isn't merely a lack of attention or an excess of hyperactivity, but a fundamental impairment in several interconnected cognitive functions. These deficits profoundly impact an individual's ability to self-regulate, plan, and execute tasks effectively.

The "Deficit in Internalizing" component refers to the challenges individuals with ADHD face in processing and integrating internal cues. This isn't simply about being "in their own world," but a more nuanced difficulty in accessing and utilizing internal feedback loops vital for self-monitoring and emotional regulation. Imagine trying to write a complex essay. A neurotypical individual might internally monitor their progress, identify areas needing improvement, and adjust their writing accordingly. An individual with ADHD might struggle with this internal feedback loop, leading to difficulties in pacing, editing, and ensuring the overall coherence of their work. This deficit manifests in various ways, including difficulties with planning, organizing, and prioritizing tasks. They may struggle to initiate tasks, and even when they do, maintaining consistent effort and focus can be a major hurdle. The inability to effectively monitor one's own internal state can also lead to difficulties with emotional regulation, resulting in increased emotional lability and impulsivity. This internal disorganization often extends to difficulty managing time, leading to chronic lateness or missed deadlines. Examples could include forgetting appointments, misplacing items frequently, or struggling to meet work or academic deadlines despite sufficient time and resources. The impact on personal relationships can also be significant, leading to frustration and conflict due to poor communication and organization.

The "Vigilance" component of the DIVA model addresses the difficulty individuals with ADHD experience in maintaining sustained attention and alertness. This isn't simply about distractibility, but a deeper-seated difficulty in sustaining focus over time. Think of it as a fluctuating attentional spotlight—bright and focused at times, but prone to dimming or shifting unexpectedly. This makes sustained attention to demanding tasks exceptionally challenging. This explains why individuals with ADHD may struggle in situations requiring prolonged concentration, such as lectures, meetings, or reading lengthy documents. They may find themselves easily distracted by external stimuli or internal thoughts, leading to difficulties in completing tasks requiring sustained effort. It's not just a matter of willpower; it's a neurological challenge affecting the brain's ability to maintain a consistent level of arousal and focus. This vigilance deficit contributes significantly to academic and professional challenges, hindering their ability to acquire new skills and maintain performance over extended periods. The impact extends beyond academic and professional settings. Maintaining consistent engagement in hobbies or social activities can also prove difficult, leading to feelings of frustration and isolation.

Finally, the "Attention" aspect of the DIVA model delves into the selective attention deficits often observed in ADHD. This refers to the ability to filter out irrelevant stimuli and focus on relevant information. In individuals with ADHD, this filtering mechanism is often impaired, leading to increased distractibility and difficulty concentrating in noisy or cluttered environments. Consider the experience of trying to focus on a conversation in a crowded restaurant. A neurotypical individual might be able to filter out the background noise and concentrate on the conversation. An individual with ADHD might find this significantly more challenging, constantly being drawn to other auditory or visual stimuli. This deficit extends beyond simply external distractions. Internal thoughts and worries can also become significant distractions, diverting attention away from the task at hand. This can lead to difficulties in completing tasks requiring attention to detail, impacting accuracy and efficiency. This difficulty with selective attention is further compounded by the internalizing deficit, creating a vicious cycle of difficulty staying on track. This constant battle with distraction can be incredibly exhausting, leading to feelings of overwhelm and frustration.

The interconnectedness of these three core deficits – Internalizing, Vigilance, and Attention – is a crucial aspect of the DIVA model. They are not independent entities but rather interwoven aspects of a broader neurocognitive impairment. For instance, the inability to effectively internalize feedback (Deficit in Internalizing) can lead to difficulties in maintaining vigilance (Vigilance) and effectively directing attention (Attention). The struggle to sustain attention (Vigilance) can, in turn, exacerbate difficulties with self-monitoring and self-regulation (Deficit in Internalizing), hindering the ability to strategically allocate attentional resources (Attention). This interconnectedness underscores the complexity of ADHD and highlights the need for comprehensive assessment and treatment strategies that address all aspects of the disorder.

The clinical implications of the DIVA model are significant. Understanding these deficits allows clinicians to tailor interventions more effectively. For instance, recognizing the deficit in internalizing allows for the development of strategies aimed at improving self-awareness and selfmonitoring skills. This might involve training in mindfulness techniques, self-instructional strategies, or the use of external organizational tools. Addressing the vigilance deficit might involve implementing strategies to improve sustained attention, such as breaking down tasks into smaller, more manageable chunks, using timers, or creating structured environments that minimize distractions. Finally, tackling the attention deficit might focus on enhancing selective attention skills through cognitive training exercises, mindfulness practices, and environmental modifications.

The DIVA model also sheds light on the heterogeneity of ADHD presentations. The severity and prominence of each deficit can vary considerably between individuals, leading to diverse symptom profiles. This explains why two individuals diagnosed with ADHD might exhibit very different symptoms and challenges. One individual might primarily struggle with disorganization and impulsivity (primarily internalizing and attention deficits), while another might experience more pronounced difficulties with sustained attention and distractibility (primarily vigilance and attention deficits). This understanding is crucial for personalized treatment planning. The DIVA model encourages a move away from a "one-size-fits-all" approach to treatment, emphasizing the importance of individualized interventions tailored to the unique strengths and weaknesses of each individual.

Beyond specific therapeutic techniques, the DIVA model offers a valuable framework for understanding the broader impact of ADHD on an individual's life. The model helps to explain not only the core symptoms but also the associated challenges in various areas of functioning, including academic performance, occupational success, social relationships, and emotional well-being. By recognizing the interconnected nature of the deficits, clinicians and individuals with ADHD can work together to develop targeted strategies to mitigate these challenges and improve overall quality of life. For example, understanding the internalizing deficit can help explain difficulties with emotional regulation, leading to interventions focused on emotional awareness and coping skills.

Moreover, the DIVA model can be instrumental in educating both individuals with ADHD and their families, providing a clearer understanding of the underlying neurocognitive mechanisms driving their experiences. This understanding can help to reduce feelings of self-blame and shame, promoting a more compassionate and supportive environment. It fosters a sense of agency and empowers individuals with ADHD to actively participate in their treatment and management. This collaborative approach, informed by the DIVA model, improves treatment adherence and ultimately leads to better outcomes. By understanding the intricate interplay of deficits within the DIVA model, individuals with ADHD can develop personalized strategies to navigate their daily challenges more effectively and achieve a greater sense of control over their lives. The framework, therefore, is not just a diagnostic tool; it's a powerful catalyst for self-understanding, empowerment, and improved management of ADHD symptoms.

The DIVA model's strength lies in its ability to provide a comprehensive and nuanced understanding of ADHD, moving beyond simplistic symptom checklists and offering a deeper insight into the underlying neurocognitive mechanisms. It fosters a more holistic and individualized approach to treatment, moving away from a solely pharmacological focus and towards a more integrated approach that incorporates both pharmacological and nonpharmacological interventions, addressing the specific challenges faced by each individual. This emphasis on personalization is critical for effective long-term management and improved quality of life for those living with ADHD. Through understanding the interplay of the internalizing, vigilance, and attention deficits, clinicians and individuals can collaborate to develop tailored strategies that address the unique challenges presented by this multifaceted condition. The next chapter will delve into the specifics of these interventions, illustrating how the DIVA model informs practical treatment approaches.

References

ADHD C: Understanding and Managing Attention Deficit Hyperactivity Disorder | A Simplified Psychology Guide. https://psychology.tips/adhd-c/

Blog of Paola Bailey, Psy.D.. https://www.paolabailey.com/blog_old

Why Human Transcription Service is Preferred. https://www.gte-media.com/why-human-transcription-service-is-preferred/

Debunking Myths About ADHD: What Everyone Needs to Know. https://myworldgo.com/blog/74522/debunking-myths-about-adhd-what-everyone-needs-to-know

The Relationship Between Social Anxiety and Substance Use. https://blog.compasshealthcenter.net/the-relationship-between-social-anxiety-and-substance-use

2. Business Strategy/Structure Archives - My TrueNORTH UK. https://www.mytruenorth.biz/category/business-strategy-structure/

Family Therapy for Coping with Chronic Illness in Portland. https://firstbasegloves.net/family-therapy-for-coping-with-chronic-illness-in-portland/

ADHD's Effect on Memory Functioning: Overcoming Obstacles and Putting Effective Techniques in Place - About Blavida.com. https://blavida.com/adhds-effect-on-memory-functioning-overcoming-obstacles-and-putting-effective-techniques-in-place/

AI in Healthcare: Transforming Diagnosis and Treatment for Better Patient Care - Whisper Wagon Wire. https://whisperwagonwire.com/ai-in-healthcare-transforming-diagnosis-and-treatment-for-better-patient-care/

COVID-19 Auto Industry Resources | Coronavirus Resources - 5 Fold Agency. https://5fold.agency/coronavirus-resources

5

Differential Diagnosis of Adult ADHD

Accurate diagnosis of Adult ADHD requires a meticulous process of differentiation from other conditions that share overlapping symptoms. Many disorders present with symptoms that can easily be confused with those of ADHD, leading to misdiagnosis and inappropriate treatment. This section will delve into the crucial aspect of differential diagnosis, highlighting the importance of comprehensive assessment and the exclusion of other potential contributing factors. Failing to differentiate ADHD from other conditions can result in ineffective treatment strategies and a significant impact on the individual's quality of life.

One of the most common conditions frequently confused with ADHD is anxiety. Both conditions can manifest with restlessness, difficulty concentrating, and irritability. However, the underlying mechanisms differ significantly. Anxiety is characterized by excessive worry, fear, and apprehension, often accompanied by physical symptoms such as rapid heartbeat, shortness of breath, and muscle tension. While individuals with ADHD may experience anxiety as a comorbid condition, the core symptoms of ADHD focus on inattention, hyperactivity, and impulsivity, even in the absence of overt anxiety triggers. A thorough diagnostic evaluation should explore the temporal relationship between symptoms—does anxiety precede or follow the presentation of ADHD symptoms? The presence of specific anxiety-related symptoms, such as panic attacks or phobias, would further differentiate the two. Utilizing standardized anxiety scales, such as the Generalized Anxiety Disorder 7-item (GAD-7) scale, alongside ADHD rating scales, can provide a clearer picture and aid in differential diagnosis.

Depression often presents with symptoms that overlap significantly with those of ADHD. Fatigue, difficulty concentrating, and lack of motivation are common to both conditions. However, the pervasive sense of sadness, hopelessness, and loss of interest in previously enjoyed activities are key distinguishing features of depression. Furthermore, sleep disturbances in depression often manifest as insomnia or hypersomnia, differing from the sleep difficulties often observed in ADHD, which might involve difficulty falling asleep or staying asleep, but not necessarily consistent with a major depressive episode. Again, structured diagnostic interviews, such as the Patient Health Questionnaire-9 (PHQ-9) for depression, are essential tools alongside ADHD assessments for accurate differentiation. It is crucial to note that the comorbidity of ADHD and depression is very common. It's not a matter of either/or but rather identifying the primary diagnosis and addressing both conditions accordingly.

Substance use disorders are another significant area for differential diagnosis. Stimulant use can mimic the hyperactivity and impulsivity characteristic of ADHD, while sedative use might mask the inattention and hyperactivity, potentially leading to a delayed or missed diagnosis. The presence of substance use, especially chronic misuse, needs to be carefully assessed through detailed substance use history taking, coupled with toxicological screening, as appropriate. The pattern and context of symptom presentation are crucial. For instance, symptoms associated with substance withdrawal could be mistaken for the presentation of ADHD. A detailed history focusing on the timeline of symptom onset and the relationship to substance use is critical in this differentiation.

Other conditions that require consideration include oppositional defiant disorder (ODD), conduct disorder (CD), and autism spectrum disorder (ASD). ODD is characterized by a persistent pattern of negativistic, defiant, and hostile behavior towards authority figures, which can manifest as disruptive behaviour that might be mistaken for hyperactivity in ADHD. However, unlike ADHD, ODD lacks the core features of inattention and impulsivity that are central to the ADHD diagnosis. Conduct disorder involves a more severe pattern of violation of the basic rights of others and age-appropriate societal norms, presenting with behaviors such as aggression, theft, and vandalism. While ADHD can coexist with CD, the presence of serious antisocial behaviour is a clear differentiator.

Autism spectrum disorder (ASD) presents challenges in differential diagnosis due to shared symptoms such as inattention and difficulties with social interaction. However, ASD involves difficulties with communication, repetitive behaviors, and restricted interests, often emerging in early childhood, distinguishing it from

ADHD. Comprehensive assessment, often involving multiple professionals, is crucial in distinguishing these conditions, focusing on the developmental history and the profile of symptoms.

Obsessive-compulsive disorder (OCD) and other anxiety related disorders might show some overlap with ADHD. While both OCD and ADHD can manifest with problems focusing, the symptoms in OCD stem from intrusive thoughts and compulsions, whereas ADHD symptoms stem from underlying neurobiological deficits in attention and impulse control.

Sleep disorders can also mimic ADHD symptoms. Poor sleep hygiene, sleep apnea, or other sleep disturbances can lead to fatigue, difficulty concentrating, and irritability, mimicking some symptoms of ADHD. A detailed sleep history and polysomnography, if necessary, can help identify any underlying sleep problems that may be contributing to the observed symptoms.

Beyond specific disorders, other factors can contribute to symptoms that resemble ADHD. These include head injuries, brain tumors, and other neurological conditions. A thorough neurological examination and neuropsychological testing are often crucial to rule out such conditions. Furthermore, certain medications, particularly stimulant medications used to treat other disorders, can produce side effects that resemble symptoms of ADHD. A detailed medication history is crucial in this context.

The diagnostic process for ADHD in adults therefore requires a comprehensive approach, including a detailed clinical interview, review of developmental history, use of standardized rating scales (like the Conner's Adult ADHD Rating Scales, Wender Utah Rating Scale, etc.), and potentially, neuropsychological testing. Collateral information from family members, partners, or colleagues can be invaluable in corroborating self-reported information and establishing a more comprehensive picture. It's vital to assess for comorbid conditions, using validated tools to diagnose depression, anxiety, substance use, and other relevant conditions. This multi-pronged approach not only identifies ADHD but also clarifies the presence and nature of any co-occurring conditions that necessitate simultaneous treatment. By systematically considering and ruling out these potential alternative diagnoses, clinicians can ensure an accurate diagnosis of ADHD and initiate appropriate, individualized interventions. The goal is not simply to label the condition but to tailor treatment plans that address the unique combination of symptoms and challenges faced by each individual. This collaborative approach, integrating subjective reports with objective assessment data, provides the best chance for successful outcomes. The complexity of ADHD, its often intricate relationship with other conditions, and the need for personalized treatment underscore the critical role of a comprehensive differential diagnosis process.

References

HYPNO-BLOG - CANADIAN HYPNOTHERAPY METAPHYSICS SPIRITUALITY OTTAWA. https://www.chmsottawa.com/hypnoblog/understanding-managing-anxiety

What is the best treatment for mental health in NSW?. https://malabarmedicalcentre.com.au/what-is-the-best-treatment-for-mental-health-in-nsw/

Children Behavior Disorders – Frolics Of Hope Africa. https://www.frolicsafrica.org/children-behavior-disorders/

Bipolar vs Borderline Personality Disorder (BPD). https://www.katiereed.com/bipolar-vs-borderline-personality-disorder-bpd/

6

The Role of Self Report Measures and Collateral Information in Diagnosis

Building upon the comprehensive diagnostic process outlined previously, we now delve into the crucial roles of self-report measures and collateral information in achieving an accurate diagnosis of adult ADHD. While the clinical interview provides invaluable qualitative data and allows for a nuanced understanding of the individual's subjective experience, it is insufficient on its own. The complexities of ADHD, its overlap with other conditions, and the inherent biases present in self-reporting necessitate a multi-faceted approach that incorporates objective data and perspectives from multiple sources.

Self-report measures, standardized questionnaires designed to assess ADHD symptoms, offer a crucial objective element to the diagnostic process. These instruments provide a structured and quantifiable assessment of symptom severity and frequency, minimizing the potential for subjective biases that may influence clinical judgment. Several widely used scales exist, each with its own strengths and weaknesses. The Adult ADHD Self-Report Scale (ASRS) is a commonly employed screening tool, readily accessible and relatively quick to administer. It provides a concise assessment of core

ADHD symptoms, aiding in identifying individuals who warrant further evaluation. However, its brevity may limit its sensitivity in capturing the full spectrum of ADHD's multifaceted presentation.

The Conners' Adult ADHD Rating Scales (CAARS) offer a more comprehensive assessment, encompassing a broader range of symptoms including inattention, hyperactivity, impulsivity, and associated emotional and behavioral difficulties. The CAARS also incorporates self-report and informant (collateral) versions, allowing for a comparison between the individual's perspective and that of someone who regularly observes them. Discrepancies between these reports can provide valuable insights, highlighting potential areas for further exploration and clarifying the presence of potential biases. For instance, an individual might downplay their inattentiveness due to self-awareness or an ingrained coping mechanism, while a spouse might readily observe and report its impact on daily functioning.

Other noteworthy self-report measures include the Wender Utah Rating Scale (WURS), which focuses on retrospective assessment of childhood symptoms, and the ADHD Rating Scale-IV (ADHD-RS-IV), which assesses symptoms across various settings. The choice of a specific instrument often depends on the clinical context, the specific information sought, and the overall diagnostic approach. It is crucial to understand the limitations of each scale, acknowledging that these instruments are not diagnostic tools in themselves but rather valuable components within a comprehensive assessment strategy.

The importance of collateral information cannot be overstated. Gathering information from individuals who know the patient well—such as spouses, family members, close friends, or colleagues—provides a crucial external perspective, often revealing patterns of behavior and symptoms that may not be readily apparent during a single clinical interview. This perspective offers a valuable check on the individual's self-report, mitigating the potential for underreporting or misinterpretation of symptoms. For example, an individual might not be fully aware of the impact of their impulsivity on their workplace performance, while a colleague might readily observe instances of interrupting, poor task completion, or difficulty with organizational tasks.

The process of obtaining collateral information requires sensitivity and ethical considerations. It's imperative to obtain informed consent from the individual before contacting other informants. Clinicians should carefully explain the purpose of obtaining collateral information, emphasizing its importance in ensuring an accurate diagnosis and developing a tailored treatment plan. They should also address any concerns the individual may have regarding privacy and confidentiality. The collected information should be treated with the utmost respect and confidentiality, adhering to all relevant ethical guidelines.

Integrating self-report and collateral information necessitates careful consideration and interpretation. While consistency between self-report and collateral information strengthens the diagnostic confidence, discrepancies require further investigation. Discrepancies might stem from several factors, including:

Self-awareness and denial: Individuals with ADHD may minimize their symptoms due to a lack of awareness or a defense mechanism against admitting struggles.

Observer bias: Informants may have their own biases, interpretations, or motivations that affect their reporting.

Symptom variability: ADHD symptoms can fluctuate over time and across different settings, leading to inconsistencies in reporting.

Comorbid conditions: Co-occurring conditions like anxiety or depression can complicate the picture and influence both self-report and collateral accounts.

Addressing discrepancies requires a detailed clinical interview focused on identifying potential contributing factors and obtaining clarification. Further assessments, including neuropsychological testing or additional rating scales focusing on specific aspects of the suspected comorbid condition, may be necessary. The clinical judgment of the practitioner, based on their experience and knowledge, plays a vital role in interpreting the data, weighing the different perspectives, and arriving at a holistic understanding.

The integration of self-report and collateral information is not simply about adding numerical scores or confirming the individual's own perception. It's a crucial process for building a comprehensive clinical picture that considers various perspectives, assesses symptom variability, and identifies potential confounding factors. By incorporating multiple data points and engaging in a thoughtful interpretation of the information gathered, clinicians enhance the accuracy of their diagnosis and increase the likelihood of developing effective and personalized treatment plans. This approach highlights the fundamental shift away from a purely symptom-based diagnosis toward a more holistic understanding of the individual's experience, functioning, and the impact of ADHD on their daily life.

In conclusion, a robust diagnosis of adult ADHD relies heavily on a well-integrated approach that thoughtfully incorporates both self-report measures and collateral information. The strengths of each method are complementary, offsetting potential limitations and biases. This multi-pronged approach contributes significantly to minimizing diagnostic errors, reducing the possibility of misdiagnosis, and ensuring that the developed treatment plan accurately addresses the unique challenges faced by the individual. It's a crucial step in fostering a better understanding of ADHD and improving the lives of those affected by this complex condition. The ultimate goal remains the development of a personalized and effective treatment strategy that addresses the specific needs of the individual, improving their overall well-being and quality of life. The process should not only aim to identify ADHD but also to understand its impact on various aspects of the individual's life, taking into account their unique strengths, challenges, and aspirations. This comprehensive approach forms the cornerstone of effective and compassionate care for adults with ADHD.

Only through this meticulous process can we ensure that treatment plans are tailored to the specific needs of each individual, maximizing the chances of positive outcomes and improving their overall quality of life. The continued development and refinement of diagnostic tools and strategies are essential to improve the accuracy and efficiency of ADHD diagnosis, paving the way for more effective and personalized interventions

References

Autism and Addiction's Close Connection. https://www.magnetaba.com/blog/autism-and-addictions-close-connection

7

Inattention and Its Manifestations in Adults

Inattention, a core symptom of ADHD, manifests differently in adults than in children. While hyperactivity and impulsivity may lessen with age, inattention often persists, subtly yet significantly impacting various aspects of adult life. Unlike the hyperactive child easily identified in a classroom, the inattentive adult might blend seamlessly into their environment, their struggles often unrecognized or misattributed. This section will delve into the multifaceted nature of inattention in adults with ADHD, exploring its diverse manifestations and providing practical strategies for management.

One key characteristic of inattention in adults with ADHD is difficulty sustaining attention to tasks requiring prolonged focus. This isn't simply a matter of being easily distracted; it's a fundamental struggle with maintaining concentration, even when genuinely interested in the task at hand. Imagine an adult attempting to complete a complex work project. While they might initially be engaged, their attention gradually wanes, leading to frequent shifts in focus, unfinished tasks, and a feeling of being overwhelmed. They may start a project with enthusiasm, only to find themselves hours later, having accomplished little, their attention diverted by seemingly minor distractions – a notification on their phone, a passing thought, or a sound from the next room. This isn't laziness or lack of motivation; it's a neurological challenge affecting their ability to maintain consistent cognitive effort.

This difficulty with sustained attention often translates into significant challenges in the workplace. Adults with ADHD might struggle to complete projects on time, miss deadlines, and experience difficulty organizing their workload. They may struggle to prioritize tasks, leading to a sense of constant overwhelm and a feeling of being perpetually behind. The inability to filter out irrelevant stimuli can make focusing in a busy office environment particularly challenging, leading to reduced productivity and increased stress. Furthermore, the tendency to lose track of details can result in errors and missed opportunities, potentially impacting career progression and job satisfaction. For example, a lawyer might miss crucial details in a case file, an accountant might make calculation errors, or a writer might fail to proofread their work adequately. These seemingly minor errors can have significant consequences.

The impact of inattention extends beyond the professional sphere. Managing household chores, paying bills on time, and even maintaining personal hygiene can become significant struggles. Simple tasks that most adults accomplish effortlessly can become monumental efforts, resulting in feelings of frustration, inadequacy, and a sense of being overwhelmed. This constant battle against disorganization and forgetfulness can lead to considerable stress and negatively impact self-esteem. For instance, an individual might struggle to keep their home organized, leading to feelings of shame and embarrassment when visitors arrive. They might repeatedly forget appointments or misplace important documents, causing additional stress and anxiety.

Relationships can also be significantly affected by inattention. Partners and family members may become frustrated by missed appointments, forgotten promises, and a perceived lack of attention or attentiveness. The individual with ADHD may struggle to follow conversations, miss social cues, or fail to fully engage in family activities. This can lead to feelings of isolation, misunderstanding, and conflict within the relationship. The constant need for reminders and the frequent apologies for forgetfulness can erode the relationship over time, creating distance and resentment. Conversations might feel one-sided as the individual with ADHD struggles to maintain focus, leading to the other party feeling unheard or unimportant.

The challenges posed by inattention extend to mental health. The constant struggle to stay organized, complete tasks, and manage daily responsibilities can lead to feelings of anxiety, depression, and low self-esteem. The frustration of failing to meet self-imposed expectations can be particularly damaging, contributing to a sense of inadequacy and selfcriticism. The feeling of perpetually falling short can create a cycle of negative self-perception, leading to feelings of hopelessness and despair. Furthermore, the inattention may lead to procrastination and avoidance of tasks, perpetuating the cycle of overwhelm and frustration.

However, understanding inattention as a core symptom of ADHD is crucial for effective management. The first step is recognizing the pattern and identifying situations where inattention is most pronounced. Keeping a journal or using a daily planner can help track these patterns and identify triggers. Once these patterns are identified, specific strategies can be implemented to mitigate their impact. These strategies are multifaceted and address multiple aspects of life.

One important strategy is environmental modification. Minimizing distractions is essential. This might involve creating a dedicated workspace free from clutter and interruptions, using noise-canceling headphones, or turning off notifications on electronic devices. Creating a structured environment reduces the cognitive load and makes focusing on tasks easier. Simple changes, like decluttering a workspace or using a timer to break tasks into smaller, manageable chunks, can have a profound impact on the ability to maintain attention.

Another effective strategy is behavioral management techniques. These techniques, often incorporated into cognitive behavioral therapy (CBT), involve identifying and addressing maladaptive behaviors associated with inattention. Techniques like self-monitoring, reinforcement of positive behaviors, and breaking down tasks into smaller, manageable steps can greatly improve focus and concentration. This may involve establishing clear goals, breaking down large tasks into smaller, more achievable steps, and utilizing time management tools such as planners or apps to aid in organization and task prioritization.

Furthermore, mindfulness and meditation practices can enhance attention and reduce impulsivity. Regular mindfulness exercises, such as focusing on the breath or bodily sensations, can improve concentration and reduce the impact of distracting thoughts. Meditation helps train the brain to stay present and focused, reducing the tendency to wander off. The practice of mindfulness helps to cultivate present-moment awareness, decreasing the likelihood of being overwhelmed by external stimuli and improving one's capacity for sustained attention.

Pharmacological interventions also play a crucial role in managing inattention. Stimulant and non-stimulant medications can significantly improve attention and focus. These medications work by modulating neurotransmitter activity in the brain, improving the ability to concentrate and reducing impulsivity. However, it's crucial to note that medication alone is insufficient; it should be used in conjunction with behavioral strategies and lifestyle modifications for optimal results. The selection and dosage of medication should always be determined in consultation with a healthcare professional and tailored to the individual's needs and response.

Finally, seeking social support is essential. Joining support groups or connecting with others who have ADHD can provide valuable emotional support and practical advice. Sharing experiences with others who understand the challenges of inattention can reduce feelings of isolation and foster a sense of community. Open communication with family members and friends is also crucial to building understanding and fostering supportive relationships. Educating loved ones about the nature of ADHD and its impact on attention can improve interpersonal relationships and create a more supportive environment.

In conclusion, inattention in adults with ADHD is a multifaceted challenge with far-reaching consequences. However, with a comprehensive approach encompassing environmental modifications, behavioral strategies, mindfulness practices, pharmacological interventions, and social support, individuals can effectively manage their symptoms and lead fulfilling lives. Understanding the nature of inattention and its impact is the first step towards gaining control and building a more manageable and productive life. The journey requires patience, persistence, and a willingness to explore various strategies to find what works best for each individual. The goal is not to eliminate inattention entirely but to learn effective strategies to navigate its challenges and minimize its negative impacts on daily life.

References

What can help you beside INCUP with ADHD? | Dotneteers.net. https://dotneteers.net/what-can-help-you-beside-incup-with-adhd/

Mastering Time Management: A Student's Guide to Balancing Academics and Life. https://foreverbreak.com/guest/student-time-management/

Empathy Overwhelm, What Is It And How To Overcome It. https://www.higherperspectives.com/empathy-overwhelm-what-is-it-and-how-to-overcome-it.html

8

Hyperactivity and Impulsivity in Adult ADHD

While inattention often forms the most prominent and persistent challenge for many adults with ADHD, the symptoms of hyperactivity and impulsivity, though potentially less overt than in childhood, continue to exert a significant influence on daily life. Understanding their nuanced manifestations in adulthood is crucial for accurate diagnosis and effective management. Unlike the boisterous hyperactivity commonly associated with childhood ADHD, these symptoms often transform and subtly impact various aspects of adult functioning.

Hyperactivity in adults rarely presents as the constant physical restlessness seen in children. Instead, it often manifests as internal restlessness, an inability to sit still for extended periods, a feeling of being "wired," or an incessant need to be doing something – anything – to alleviate this internal pressure. This can lead to a chronic state of fidgeting, pacing, or an overwhelming urge to multitask, often leading to decreased efficiency and unfinished projects. Imagine trying to focus during a long meeting, feeling the internal pressure building as the quiet hum of the conference room amplifies the feeling of needing to move, to escape the stillness. This internal hyperactivity can be profoundly exhausting, leading to burnout and impacting relationships as the individual struggles to manage their own internal experience.

It's important to distinguish between this internal restlessness and simply being energetic. While energy is a positive attribute, the hyperactivity experienced in ADHD often feels qualitatively different; it's less a productive energy and more a chaotic, internally driven pressure that interferes with focus and task completion. It's the constant mental buzzing that makes it difficult to settle into quiet activities or concentrate on a single task. This can lead to difficulties in maintaining a consistent work routine, staying organized, and managing time effectively, contributing to significant stress and frustration. The inability to regulate this internal state can manifest in impulsive behaviors, further compounding the challenges faced by individuals with ADHD.

Impulsivity, another core symptom, presents in various forms in adults with ADHD. While impulsive behaviors in children might be characterized by immediate, often disruptive actions, adult impulsivity is frequently more subtle yet equally impactful. It can manifest as reckless decision-making, a tendency to act without considering the consequences, or difficulty inhibiting responses. For example, an adult with ADHD might impulsively overspend, make rash decisions in relationships, or engage in risky behaviors without fully appreciating the potential risks involved. This impulsive nature can profoundly impact different areas of life, leading to financial instability, strained relationships, and even legal repercussions.

One common manifestation of impulsivity in adults with ADHD is emotional impulsivity. This refers to a tendency to react emotionally without filtering or considering the context of the situation. An individual might experience sudden outbursts of anger or frustration, making it difficult to navigate challenging situations calmly and rationally. This emotional reactivity can significantly strain relationships, both personal and professional, creating misunderstandings and damaging connections. The lack of emotional regulation can leave individuals feeling overwhelmed and out of control, further exacerbating their struggles.

Another often overlooked aspect of impulsivity in adults with ADHD is the tendency towards interrupting conversations. While this may seem like a minor issue, frequently interrupting others can be socially disruptive and damage professional relationships. It stems from an inability to regulate the urge to express thoughts immediately, often overshadowing other individuals' contributions. This behavior can be easily misinterpreted as rudeness or disinterest, hindering communication and collaboration.

The challenge in recognizing and managing hyperactivity and impulsivity lies in differentiating these behaviors from other conditions or simply a personality trait. Many people are naturally energetic or prone to occasional impulsive acts. The key difference in ADHD lies in the frequency, intensity, and pervasive nature of these symptoms, impacting multiple aspects of life and causing significant impairment. For instance, occasional impulsive spending is common, but consistent financial instability due to uncontrolled spending patterns might indicate an underlying ADHD-related impulsivity issue. Similarly, occasional irritability is normal, but frequent and disproportionate emotional outbursts might highlight an emotional impulsivity problem.

The diagnostic process requires careful consideration of the individual's history, behavioral patterns, and the impact of these behaviors on their daily life. Clinicians often rely on both self-reported questionnaires, such as the Adult ADHD Self-Report Scale (ASRS), and collateral information from family members or colleagues to gain a comprehensive understanding of the individual's symptoms. This holistic approach is crucial to avoid misdiagnosis and ensure that treatment is tailored to the specific needs of the individual.

Managing hyperactivity and impulsivity in adults with

ADHD requires a multi-pronged approach. Pharmacological interventions, such as stimulant or non-stimulant medications, can be highly effective in reducing hyperactivity and improving impulse control. These medications work by modulating neurotransmitter levels in the brain, helping to improve focus and attention. However, medication is often most effective when combined with nonpharmacological strategies.

Behavioral therapies, such as Cognitive Behavioral Therapy (CBT) and behavioral activation, play a crucial role in teaching individuals strategies for managing their impulsive behaviors and regulating their emotions. CBT helps individuals identify and challenge negative thought patterns that contribute to impulsive actions, while behavioral activation focuses on increasing engagement in rewarding activities to reduce reliance on impulsive behaviors for emotional regulation.

Lifestyle modifications also play a significant role in managing hyperactivity and impulsivity. Regular exercise can help reduce internal restlessness and improve mood regulation. Mindfulness practices, such as meditation or yoga, can enhance self-awareness and promote emotional regulation. Adequate sleep is essential for managing impulsive behaviors, as sleep deprivation exacerbates both hyperactivity and impulsivity.

Establishing structured routines and utilizing organizational tools can significantly improve daily functioning. Creating clear schedules, using planners or reminder apps, and breaking down large tasks into smaller, more manageable steps can reduce feelings of overwhelm and improve task completion. Learning time management techniques, such as the Pomodoro Technique, can help improve focus and reduce the tendency to jump from one task to another.

Social support is crucial in managing the challenges of ADHD. Joining support groups or connecting with others who understand the challenges of living with ADHD can provide a sense of community and reduce feelings of isolation. Open communication with family and friends can help build understanding and foster a supportive environment. Seeking professional guidance from a therapist or counselor can provide additional emotional support and coping strategies.

It's essential to emphasize that managing hyperactivity and impulsivity is an ongoing process, not a cure. There will be good days and bad days, and individuals will need to continually adapt their strategies as their needs change. The goal is not to eliminate these symptoms entirely but to develop effective strategies to mitigate their impact on daily life and improve overall well-being. With a comprehensive approach that combines medication, therapy, lifestyle modifications, and social support, adults with ADHD can learn to manage their symptoms and live fulfilling and productive lives. The journey requires patience, perseverance, and a willingness to experiment with different strategies to find what works best for each individual. The key lies in recognizing the unique manifestations of hyperactivity and impulsivity in adulthood and developing a personalized plan to address these challenges effectively. This proactive approach fosters self-acceptance, empowers individuals to take control of their lives, and ultimately enhances their overall quality of life.

References

Self-Destructive Borderline Personality Disorder | Dr. Arceo Psychiatric Service. https://www.drarceopsychiatricservices.com/borderline-personality-disorder.php

Attention Deficit Hyperactivity Disorder: A Helpful Guide. https://calmingself.com/blog/attention-deficit-hyperactivity-disorder/

Is Ritalin Addictive? | Addiction Treatment | College Station, TX. https://brazosvalleyrehab.com/is-ritalin-addictive/

Yan, M., Shi, Y., Su, C., He, J., Li, J., Wu, N., Ye, S., Shi, Y., Zhou, C., Li, Z., Ding, X., Wang, R., & Feng,

Y. (2023). Cognitive behavioral therapy combined with head and face tuina/massage for negative emotions and sleep disorders in patients with protracted withdrawal symptoms: A study protocol for a randomized controlled trial. Research Square (Research Square). https://doi.org/10.21203/rs.3.rs-2790059/v1

Social Anxiety Therapy Toronto | Therapy Techniques for Anxiety. https://kdwellness.ca/therapy-for-anxiety-and-stress/

How Exercise Improves Mental Well-Being - A Holistic Approach to Inner Balance -. https://www.treeet.com/how-exercise-improves-mental-well-being/

How Internet Usage Can Help Alleviate Loneliness in Older Hearing Aid Wearers || TinyEYE Therapy Services. https://tinyeye.com/blog/how-internet-usage-can-help-alleviate-loneliness-in-older-hearing-aid-wearers.php

9

Emotional Dysregulation and ADHD

Building upon our understanding of hyperactivity and impulsivity in adult ADHD, we now turn to another significant and often debilitating symptom cluster: emotional dysregulation. While inattention and executive dysfunction are frequently the presenting complaints, the emotional turmoil experienced by many individuals with ADHD significantly impacts their relationships, work performance, and overall well-being. This emotional rollercoaster isn't simply a matter of occasional mood swings; it's a pervasive pattern of difficulty managing and responding to emotions in a healthy and adaptive way.

The term "emotional dysregulation" encompasses a range of experiences, from heightened irritability and easily triggered anger to intense emotional swings, low frustration tolerance, and difficulty calming oneself down after an emotional outburst. These challenges stem from a complex interplay of factors, including neurobiological differences in the brain's emotional processing centers, the impact of executive function deficits on emotional self-regulation, and the cumulative effects of past negative experiences.

One of the most common manifestations of emotional dysregulation in adults with ADHD is heightened irritability. This isn't merely a tendency to be grumpy or easily annoyed; it's a profound sensitivity to perceived slights, frustrations, and setbacks. Even minor inconveniences – a delayed train, a misplaced key, a slow-loading computer – can trigger intense feelings of anger and frustration, often disproportionate to the actual event. This irritability can strain personal relationships, leading to conflict and damaged bonds. It can also significantly affect work performance, hindering productivity and collaboration. Imagine an individual struggling to complete a complex project, already under pressure to meet a deadline. A seemingly trivial obstacle – a missing file, a technical glitch – might trigger an outburst of anger, disrupting the workflow and impacting the quality of their work. The irritability isn't intentional; it's a symptom of an underlying neurological vulnerability.

Closely related to irritability is low frustration tolerance. This refers to the difficulty in enduring challenges, setbacks, or delays without becoming overwhelmed by negative emotions. Tasks that require sustained effort, attention to detail, or persistence can be particularly challenging. The individual might start a project with enthusiasm but quickly abandon it when faced with obstacles, feeling overwhelmed by frustration and a sense of inadequacy. This can manifest in various ways, from procrastination and avoidance to impulsive behavior designed to escape the frustrating situation. For example, an individual might start a home improvement project but quickly lose motivation when confronted with unexpected complications. Instead of persevering, they might abandon the project entirely, leaving it unfinished, or they might impulsively purchase expensive tools they don't really need, in an attempt to compensate for their frustration and perceived lack of progress.

Another key aspect of emotional dysregulation in ADHD is emotional lability. This refers to the experience of rapid and unpredictable shifts in mood. Individuals with ADHD may experience intense joy one moment and profound sadness or anger the next, often with little or no discernible trigger. This emotional volatility can be confusing and distressing, both for the individual experiencing it and for those around them. This emotional unpredictability can make it difficult to form and maintain stable relationships, as others struggle to understand and respond to the rapidly shifting emotional landscape. A seemingly inconsequential event – a compliment, a simple question, a piece of feedback – might trigger a dramatic shift in mood, leaving the individual and those around them feeling disoriented and uncertain. The rapid and often inexplicable nature of these emotional swings can lead to feelings of isolation and shame.

The impact of these emotional challenges extends beyond interpersonal relationships and work productivity. Emotional dysregulation can significantly affect self-esteem and self perception. Individuals who struggle to manage their emotions may experience a sense of inadequacy, shame, and self-criticism. They may internalize negative feedback, viewing themselves as flawed, unstable, and incapable of managing their own emotions. This self-criticism can exacerbate existing feelings of frustration and anger, creating a vicious cycle of negative emotions and self-doubt. They might be their own harshest critics, focusing on mistakes and imperfections while overlooking accomplishments and strengths.

However, it's crucial to understand that these emotional experiences are not a character flaw or a sign of weakness. They are symptoms of a neurological condition that affects the brain's ability to regulate emotions. This understanding is paramount for self-compassion and effective management strategies.

Fortunately, various techniques can help individuals with ADHD manage their emotional dysregulation. These strategies, often integrated within a broader treatment plan, focus on developing emotional awareness, improving coping skills, and fostering self-compassion.

Mindfulness practices, such as meditation and deep breathing exercises, can help individuals become more aware of their emotions as they arise, without judgment. By cultivating this awareness, they can learn to identify triggers, understand the intensity of their emotional responses, and develop strategies to manage them before they escalate. Regular mindfulness practice can cultivate emotional regulation skills, enhancing the capacity to respond to challenges in a more balanced and adaptive way.

Cognitive Behavioral Therapy (CBT) is another powerful tool for managing emotional dysregulation. CBT helps individuals identify and challenge negative thought patterns and beliefs that contribute to emotional distress. By learning to reframe negative thoughts and develop more adaptive coping mechanisms, individuals can reduce the intensity and frequency of their emotional outbursts. Through CBT, individuals can learn to differentiate between the event and their emotional reaction, thereby separating themselves from overwhelming emotions. This process allows for a more objective perspective, mitigating the intensity and impact of the emotional response.

Furthermore, Acceptance and Commitment Therapy (ACT) offers a valuable approach to managing emotions. ACT focuses on accepting difficult emotions as a natural part of the human experience, rather than fighting or suppressing them. Instead of trying to eliminate negative emotions, ACT encourages individuals to focus on their values and commit to actions that align with those values, even in the face of emotional distress. This acceptance-based approach helps individuals to move forward with their lives, even when experiencing challenging emotions, leading to a more resilient and fulfilling life.

Lifestyle modifications play a significant role in managing emotional dysregulation. Sufficient sleep, regular exercise, and a healthy diet can have a profound impact on mood regulation and emotional stability. These lifestyle adjustments help to optimize brain function, improving emotional control and reducing irritability. Sufficient sleep, in particular, is often overlooked but crucial for effective emotional regulation. Sleep deprivation exacerbates emotional dysregulation, increasing irritability, impulsivity, and emotional lability.

In addition to these strategies, social support is invaluable. Connecting with supportive friends, family, or support groups can provide a sense of belonging, reduce feelings of isolation, and offer practical and emotional support during challenging times. Open communication with loved ones about the challenges of ADHD and emotional dysregulation can foster understanding and empathy, reducing the strain on relationships.

Finally, medication can be a helpful adjunct to these non pharmacological strategies. While medication doesn't directly "cure" emotional dysregulation, certain medications, such as stimulants or non-stimulant ADHD medications, can help to improve focus, reduce impulsivity, and stabilize mood, making it easier to implement and benefit from other coping strategies. The choice of medication, its dosage, and its effectiveness are determined through careful consideration with a healthcare professional. It's crucial to remember that medication is but one component of a holistic approach, working in tandem with therapy and lifestyle changes for optimal results.

The journey of managing emotional dysregulation in ADHD is a continuous process, requiring patience, self-compassion, and a commitment to developing effective coping strategies. It's essential to remember that setbacks are a normal part of this process. The goal is not to eliminate all emotional challenges but to develop the skills and resilience to navigate them effectively, leading to a more fulfilling and balanced life. With consistent effort, the right support system, and a holistic approach, individuals with ADHD can learn to manage their emotional experiences, building a life of greater emotional stability and well-being. The key lies in recognizing the cyclical nature of emotional challenges and developing a personalized toolbox of strategies to manage them proactively.

References

People who overcompensate for low self-worth often display these 10 behaviors - Hack Spirit. https://hackspirit.com/people-who-overcompensate-for-low-self-worth-often-display-these-behaviors/

Navigating the Labyrinth of Love: Unraveling the Complex Reasons Behind Relationship Failures - Solve All Problems. https://solve-all-problems.info/2024/01/26/navigating-the-labyrinth-of-love-unraveling-the-complex-reasons-behind-relationship-failures/

How To Deal With Anger When You Have Bipolar - Milwaukee WI. https://edelicahealth.com/how-to-deal-with-anger-when-you-have-bipolar/

Social Anxiety Therapy Toronto | Therapy Techniques for Anxiety. https://kdwellness.ca/therapy-for-anxiety-and-stress/

Understanding Insomnia: A Complex Sleep Disorder - Mindframe Psychiatry. https://www.mindframepsychiatry.com/blog/understanding-insomnia-a-complex-sleep-disorder

Zumba Dance Fitness: A path to better mental health and fitness. https://www.cherrydanceco.com/post/zumba-dance-fitness-a-joyful-path-to-mental-wellness-and-fitness

Mental Health Topics to Write About (2024). https://createmakewrite.com/writing/mental-health-topics-to-write-about/

A Therapist's Guide to Dysthymic Disorder - Therapy Group of DC. https://therapygroupdc.com/therapist-dc-blog/a-therapists-guide-to-dysthymic-disorder/

What Does ADHD Medication Do? • LDACA. https://www.ldaca.org/what-does-adhd-medication-do/

10

Cognitive Impairments Associated with ADHD

Building upon our understanding of the emotional landscape of ADHD, we now delve into another crucial aspect of the condition: its profound impact on cognitive functioning. While the hyperactivity and impulsivity, and the accompanying emotional dysregulation, are often the most visually apparent symptoms, the underlying cognitive impairments are arguably the most pervasive and significantly contribute to the challenges faced by individuals with ADHD. These difficulties aren't simply a matter of occasional forgetfulness or disorganization; they represent fundamental differences in how the brain processes information, plans actions, and regulates attention.

The cognitive impairments associated with ADHD are multifaceted and interconnected, affecting various aspects of daily life. Let's explore some of the key areas:

Working Memory Deficits: Working memory is the mental workspace where we temporarily hold and manipulate information. It's crucial for tasks ranging from following instructions to solving problems to understanding complex conversations. Individuals with ADHD often experience significant challenges in this domain. They might struggle to remember instructions, lose their train of thought mid sentence, or find it difficult to keep multiple pieces of information in mind simultaneously. This can manifest as difficulties with multitasking, remembering appointments, or even completing simple tasks that require a series of steps. The impact extends beyond simple tasks; for example, in academic settings, it can affect comprehension, note-taking, and essay writing. In professional settings, it can lead to errors, missed deadlines, and difficulty managing multiple projects. Imagine a surgeon needing to remember a complex sequence of steps during an operation – the implications of working memory deficits are substantial and far-reaching.

Executive Function Impairments: Executive functions are a set of higher-level cognitive processes that enable goal directed behavior. They include planning, organization, time management, inhibition (suppressing impulsive behaviors), and cognitive flexibility (shifting attention between tasks). Deficits in these areas are central to ADHD. Planning a complex project, for instance, can be immensely challenging. Individuals may struggle to break down the task into manageable steps, prioritize tasks effectively, and anticipate potential obstacles. This lack of planning often leads to procrastination and ultimately, to feelings of overwhelm and failure. Similarly, poor organization manifests in cluttered workspaces, misplaced items, and difficulty managing paperwork or digital files. Time management becomes a constant battle, with deadlines frequently missed and commitments easily forgotten.

The challenge of inhibition is equally profound. Impulsive behaviors, as we've previously discussed, are a hallmark of ADHD, but these behaviors are often driven by underlying deficits in inhibitory control. The inability to suppress unwanted thoughts or actions leads to interrupting conversations, making rash decisions, and engaging in risky behaviors. Cognitive flexibility, the ability to switch between tasks or adapt to changing circumstances, is also significantly impaired. This can make it difficult to transition between different activities, adapt to unexpected changes, or remain focused in environments with distractions. This struggle with shifting attention impacts various aspects of life, from maintaining focus during a meeting to switching between work and personal responsibilities.

Time Blindness: A closely related concept to executive dysfunction is "time blindness," a phenomenon where individuals with ADHD struggle to perceive and manage time effectively. They may have difficulty estimating how long tasks will take, underestimating deadlines, and chronically misjudging the passage of time. This contributes to procrastination, missed deadlines, and a persistent feeling of being rushed or behind schedule. The experience isn't simply a lack of awareness; it involves a fundamental difficulty in processing temporal information and planning accordingly. The consequences can extend into various areas of life, affecting academic performance, professional productivity, and personal relationships. The constant feeling of being overwhelmed by time constraints can significantly impact stress levels and overall well-being.

Attentional Difficulties: While inattention is a core symptom of ADHD, it's important to understand its specific cognitive underpinnings. The challenges aren't simply a lack of focus or concentration; they involve deficits in sustained attention, selective attention, and divided attention. Sustained attention refers to the ability to maintain focus on a task over a prolonged period. Individuals with ADHD often experience difficulty sustaining attention, leading to frequent mind-wandering and difficulty completing tasks. Selective attention refers to the ability to focus on relevant information while ignoring distractions. This is significantly impaired in ADHD, making it difficult to concentrate in noisy or stimulating environments. Divided attention, the ability to attend to multiple tasks simultaneously, is also challenging. Attempting to multitask often leads to decreased efficiency and increased errors, contributing to feelings of frustration and inadequacy.

Impact on Daily Life: The cognitive impairments described above have a significant impact on various aspects of daily life. Academically, they can lead to difficulties with learning, completing assignments, and taking exams. Professionally, they can affect productivity, job performance, and career advancement. In personal relationships, these cognitive challenges can contribute to difficulties with communication, organization, and managing responsibilities within the household. Financial management can also be significantly impacted, leading to difficulties with budgeting, debt management, and financial planning. The cumulative effect of these challenges can lead to significant stress, anxiety, and low self-esteem. The individual may feel constantly overwhelmed, inadequate, and unable to meet their own expectations or the expectations of others.

Compensatory Strategies: While cognitive impairments are a core feature of ADHD, many individuals develop compensatory strategies to mitigate these challenges. These strategies can be conscious or unconscious, and they can vary significantly from person to person. Some common compensatory strategies include using external organizational tools like planners, calendars, and reminder apps. Others develop meticulous systems for managing their time and tasks, breaking down complex projects into smaller, more manageable steps. Many individuals rely on visual aids, checklists, or other memory supports. Some learn to leverage their strengths, focusing on tasks that align with their cognitive abilities and delegating tasks that are more challenging. While these strategies can be effective, they often require significant effort and energy, and they may not always be sufficient to overcome the core cognitive deficits.

Cognitive Training Approaches: In recent years, there has been increasing interest in cognitive training interventions for ADHD. These approaches aim to improve specific cognitive skills, such as working memory, attention, and executive functions. Various techniques are employed, including computer-based training programs, working memory games, and mindfulness-based interventions. While the evidence base for the effectiveness of these interventions is still evolving, some studies suggest that cognitive training can lead to improvements in specific cognitive domains and potentially translate into improvements in daily functioning. It is crucial, however, to remember that cognitive training is not a standalone treatment; it's most effective when used in conjunction with other interventions, such as medication and behavioral therapy. The goal is not to "cure" ADHD but to provide tools and strategies to improve cognitive skills and manage the challenges presented by the condition.

The Interplay of Cognitive, Emotional and Behavioral Symptoms: It's crucial to recognize that the cognitive, emotional, and behavioral symptoms of ADHD are interconnected and influence one another. For instance, difficulty with working memory can lead to frustration and anxiety, which can, in turn, exacerbate impulsivity and inattention. Similarly, emotional dysregulation can impair executive functions, making it more difficult to plan, organize, and regulate behavior. This complex interplay highlights the importance of a holistic approach to treatment, addressing all aspects of the condition rather than focusing solely on individual symptoms.

Ultimately, understanding the cognitive impairments associated with ADHD is critical for effective diagnosis and treatment. It moves beyond simply labeling individuals as "inattentive" or "impulsive" to recognizing the underlying neurological mechanisms that contribute to their challenges. By understanding these cognitive difficulties, clinicians and individuals alike can develop tailored strategies to address these core issues and improve overall functioning. The journey toward effective management of ADHD requires a comprehensive approach that integrates medication, therapy, cognitive training, and adaptive strategies. The ultimate aim is not simply symptom reduction but rather the enhancement of overall well-being and quality of life. Through a combination of self-awareness, professional support, and consistent effort, individuals with ADHD can learn to harness their strengths, navigate their challenges, and live fulfilling and productive lives.

References

Akers, D. (2015). How Does Executive Function Skills Instruction Impact Student Executive Function Levels And Academic Achievement On ComCore State Standards Assessments? https://core.ac.uk/download/288064193.pdf

Attention Grabbers: Engaging Activities to Capture Your Students' Attention • DepEd Tambayan. https://depedtambayan.net/attention-grabbers-engaging-activities-capture-students-attention/

Gaume, A., Dreyfus, G., & Vialatte, F. B. (2019). A cognitive brain–computer interface monitoring sustained attentional variations during a continuous task. Cognitive Neurodynamics. https://doi.org/10.1007/s11571-019-09521-4

Cultivating Resilience: Nurturing Mental Health Among Farmers. https://www.minnwestbank.com/insights/cultivating-resilience-nurturing-mental-health-among-farmers

How to Address Burnout through Executive Coaching - HogoNext. https://hogonext.com/how-to-address-burnout-through-executive-coaching/

Mackler, J. S. (2013). The socialization of emotion regulation in late childhood: The influence of friendship. https://core.ac.uk/download/345078512.pdf

How to Utilize Cognitive Training to Delay Cognitive Decline in Early-Onset Dementia? - Regentsquare. https://regentsquare.net/archives/1789

11

The Impact of ADHD on Relationships and Social Interactions

The challenges posed by ADHD extend far beyond the individual, significantly impacting personal relationships, professional collaborations, and overall social functioning. The very traits that define the condition – impulsivity, hyperactivity, inattention, and difficulty with emotional regulation – often strain interpersonal connections, creating misunderstandings and frustrations for both the individual with ADHD and those around them. This isn't a reflection of character flaws but a consequence of neurological differences that can be understood and managed.

In romantic relationships, the impact of ADHD can be particularly profound. The difficulty with sustained attention can lead to missed anniversaries, forgotten promises, and a perceived lack of attentiveness that can be deeply hurtful to a partner. Impulsivity might manifest as sudden outbursts of anger or frustration, or perhaps a tendency towards impulsive decisions that affect the relationship without fully considering the consequences. The emotional dysregulation associated with ADHD can result in unpredictable mood swings, leaving partners feeling confused and walking on eggshells. Conversely, the partner of someone with ADHD may struggle to understand the condition, leading to accusations of laziness, carelessness, or a lack of effort. This lack of understanding can create a cycle of conflict and resentment, further eroding the relationship.

Effective communication becomes paramount in navigating these challenges. Individuals with ADHD can benefit from learning techniques to improve their listening skills, such as actively focusing on their partner's words, summarizing what they've heard, and asking clarifying questions. Partners can learn to express their needs and concerns in a calm and empathetic manner, avoiding accusatory language that can trigger defensiveness. Couples therapy, specifically tailored to address ADHD-related issues, can provide a valuable space for couples to develop strategies for better communication, conflict resolution, and mutual understanding. This may involve techniques like identifying triggers, learning to de-escalate conflicts, and developing shared coping mechanisms. Open and honest conversations about the condition, its impact, and strategies for mitigation are crucial for building a strong and supportive relationship.

Beyond romantic relationships, ADHD significantly affects friendships and family dynamics. Impulsivity can lead to damaged trust, as friends or family members might feel betrayed by unexpected actions or hurtful comments. Inattention can cause individuals with ADHD to appear disinterested or disengaged, even when they genuinely care. The struggle with emotional regulation can lead to unpredictable behaviors, straining the bonds of friendship and family. For parents with ADHD, the challenges can be particularly complex, impacting their ability to consistently meet their children's needs, enforce rules, and maintain a stable home environment. Children of parents with ADHD may struggle to understand their parent's behaviors, leading to insecurity and emotional distress.

In professional settings, the challenges presented by ADHD are equally significant. Difficulties with time management, organization, and prioritization can lead to missed deadlines, incomplete tasks, and a perceived lack of professionalism. Impulsivity can lead to inappropriate comments or actions, damaging professional relationships and hindering career advancement. The inattention associated with ADHD can make it difficult to focus during meetings, follow complex instructions, or maintain consistent performance. Furthermore, the emotional dysregulation that often accompanies ADHD can impact an individual's ability to handle stress, work effectively under pressure, or collaborate effectively with colleagues.

However, it is important to emphasize that ADHD does not preclude professional success. Many individuals with ADHD thrive in careers that leverage their strengths – creativity, innovation, and energetic enthusiasm. The key is identifying suitable work environments and implementing strategies to mitigate the challenges posed by the condition. This may involve seeking out flexible work arrangements, utilizing organizational tools such as planners and reminder apps, and developing coping mechanisms for managing stress and impulsivity. Seeking support from a mental health professional can be invaluable in developing tailored strategies for workplace success. Coaching programs specifically designed for individuals with ADHD can provide practical skills training and support in navigating professional challenges.

Social interactions, broadly speaking, also present significant hurdles. The challenges with social cues, emotional regulation, and impulse control can lead to social awkwardness, misunderstandings, and difficulties forming and maintaining social connections. Individuals with ADHD may struggle to read nonverbal cues, leading to misinterpretations of social situations. Impulsivity can lead to blurting out inappropriate comments or interrupting conversations, which can be socially damaging. Difficulty with emotional regulation can lead to unpredictable emotional responses that make social interactions challenging for both the individual with ADHD and others.

To improve social functioning, it's crucial to develop strategies for managing impulsivity, improving emotional regulation, and enhancing social skills. This can involve techniques such as mindfulness practices, cognitive behavioral therapy (CBT), and social skills training. Mindfulness techniques can help individuals become more aware of their thoughts, emotions, and impulses, allowing them to respond more thoughtfully rather than impulsively. CBT can help individuals identify negative thought patterns and replace them with more adaptive ones. Social skills training can provide structured instruction and practice in essential social skills, such as initiating conversations, engaging in active listening, and responding appropriately to social cues. Joining social groups or engaging in activities that align with personal interests can provide opportunities to practice social skills in a supportive environment.

Moreover, self-compassion plays a critical role in navigating the challenges posed by ADHD in various aspects of life. Individuals with ADHD often experience feelings of selfcriticism and inadequacy due to the challenges they face. Practicing self-compassion involves treating oneself with the same kindness and understanding that one would offer a close friend. This involves acknowledging the difficulties posed by the condition without self-blame, celebrating achievements, and focusing on progress rather than perfection. Self-compassion can empower individuals with ADHD to approach challenges with greater resilience and self-acceptance.

Finally, building a strong support network is vital. Connecting with others who understand the challenges of living with ADHD, whether through support groups, online communities, or close relationships with family and friends, can provide invaluable emotional support, practical advice, and a sense of community. Sharing experiences, learning from others, and feeling understood can significantly improve quality of life and facilitate the development of coping mechanisms. Remember that the impact of ADHD on relationships and social interactions is significant, but it's not insurmountable. By understanding the challenges posed by the condition and implementing effective strategies, individuals with ADHD can cultivate fulfilling personal relationships, thrive in their professional lives, and enjoy rich and meaningful social connections. This journey requires consistent effort, self-compassion, and a supportive environment, but the rewards of improved well-being and quality of life are substantial.

References

https://www.yourjrny.com/blogs/news/symptoms-of-adhd-in-women

How to Use Communication to Effectively Resolve Conflict. https://insights.lifemanagementsciencelabs.com/communication-and-conflict/

Benefits Of Self Therapy - Mystik Maze. https://mystikmaze.com/benefits-of-self-therapy/

12

Stimulant Medications for ADHD

Stimulant medications represent a cornerstone of pharmacological interventions for adult ADHD. Their effectiveness stems from their ability to modulate neurotransmitter systems implicated in attention, focus, and impulse control. Primarily, stimulants increase the availability of dopamine and norepinephrine in the brain's synapses. This enhanced neurotransmission helps alleviate the core symptoms of ADHD, including inattention, hyperactivity, and impulsivity. However, it's crucial to understand that the exact mechanisms by which stimulants improve ADHD symptoms are still not fully elucidated, and ongoing research continues to refine our understanding.

The two primary classes of stimulant medications used are methylphenidate and amphetamine-based drugs. Methylphenidate, available under various brand names such as Ritalin, and Concerta acts primarily by inhibiting the reuptake of dopamine and norepinephrine. This means that these neurotransmitters remain in the synaptic cleft for a longer period, leading to enhanced signaling between neurons. The duration of action varies depending on the formulation; immediate-release preparations provide shorteracting effects, while extended-release formulations offer longer-lasting symptom relief, often lasting 8-12 hours or more. This extended-release characteristic is particularly beneficial for adults who need consistent symptom management throughout the day, minimizing the need for multiple daily doses.

Amphetamine-based stimulants like Lisdexamfetamine mesilate (Elvanse), and Dexamphetamine have slightly different mechanisms of action. They also inhibit the reuptake of dopamine and norepinephrine, but they also stimulate the release of these neurotransmitters into the synapse. This dual action contributes to their efficacy in managing ADHD symptoms. Similar to methylphenidate, amphetamine formulations are available in immediate-release and extended-release forms, allowing for tailored dosing based on individual needs and responses. Vyvanse, a prodrug, undergoes conversion to dextroamphetamine in the body, providing a smoother, more gradual onset of effects compared to some other amphetamine preparations.

The choice between methylphenidate and amphetamine often depends on individual factors, including patient response, side effect profiles, and potential drug interactions. Some individuals respond better to one class of stimulants than the other. For example, a patient might experience more significant improvements in attention with methylphenidate while experiencing increased anxiety with amphetamine. Conversely, another patient might find that amphetamine provides better control of impulsivity compared to methylphenidate. Careful monitoring of response and close collaboration between the patient and prescribing physician are essential for optimal medication selection and adjustment.

Efficacy data consistently support the use of stimulant medications in adult ADHD. Numerous studies have demonstrated their effectiveness in improving attention, reducing hyperactivity and impulsivity, and enhancing overall functioning. However, it's important to note that stimulant medications are not a cure for ADHD. Rather, they are a valuable tool to help manage symptoms and improve daily life. Many individuals with ADHD find that combining medication with non-pharmacological interventions, such as therapy and lifestyle modifications, provides the most comprehensive and effective management strategy. This integrated approach addresses not only the core symptoms but also the broader impact of ADHD on various aspects of life, including work, relationships, and overall well-being.

Despite their efficacy, stimulant medications are associated with potential side effects. The most common side effects are generally mild and manageable. These include decreased appetite, insomnia, headache, and gastrointestinal upset. However, more serious side effects, though less frequent, warrant attention and potentially necessitate medication adjustment or discontinuation. These potential side effects include increased blood pressure and heart rate, anxiety, and cardiac events (although this is rare). The risk of serious cardiovascular events is typically higher in individuals with pre-existing cardiovascular conditions. Therefore, a thorough cardiovascular evaluation before initiating stimulant medication is crucial, particularly for patients with a history of heart problems or a family history of heart disease.

The management of stimulant medication side effects often involves adjustments to dosage, timing of administration, or the introduction of concomitant medications to mitigate specific side effects. For instance, insomnia might be addressed by taking the medication earlier in the day or by prescribing a low-dose sleep aid. Decreased appetite can often be managed through careful dietary planning, including frequent small meals and nutrient-dense snacks. The use of other medications to manage potentially problematic side effects, such as beta-blockers for increased heart rate, is done on a case-by-case basis.

Before initiating stimulant treatment, a comprehensive evaluation is essential. This should include a detailed assessment of the patient's medical history, including any pre-existing conditions, particularly cardiovascular disease, hypertension, or a history of substance abuse. A thorough review of current medications and potential drug interactions is crucial, as interactions can impact both the efficacy and safety of stimulant medications. The patient should be informed about the potential benefits and risks associated with stimulant medication, allowing for an informed decision-making process.

The decision to prescribe stimulant medications should be made collaboratively, involving open communication between the physician and the patient. This collaborative approach includes shared decision-making regarding medication choice, dosage, and monitoring strategies. The patient's preferences, concerns, and response to treatment should be taken into account in ongoing adjustments to the medication regimen. The treatment plan should be tailored to meet the individual needs and goals of the patient. Regular follow-up appointments are essential to monitor treatment response, adjust dosage as needed, and address any side effects.

Titration of stimulant medications is a critical aspect of effective treatment. This refers to the gradual adjustment of the medication dosage to achieve optimal symptom control while minimizing side effects. The process usually involves starting with a low dose and gradually increasing it over time, monitoring the patient's response, and adjusting accordingly. Regular assessment of symptom severity using standardized rating scales, alongside clinical observation, provides valuable information for guiding dosage adjustments. The goal is to find the lowest effective dose that provides adequate symptom relief with minimal side effects. This careful titration process is important for maximizing treatment effectiveness and minimizing the potential for adverse events.

Monitoring treatment response is an ongoing process that involves regularly assessing the patient's symptoms, both subjectively through patient reporting and objectively through observation and standardized assessment tools. The use of rating scales such as the ADHD Rating Scale (ADHD-RS) or the Conner's Adult ADHD Rating Scales (CAARS) provides a quantifiable measure of symptom severity over time, enabling a more objective evaluation of treatment effectiveness. Changes in the patient's daily functioning, such as improved work performance, better relationships, and increased organization, also provide valuable indicators of treatment success. Any significant changes in mood, sleep patterns, or other physiological parameters should also be closely monitored.

Regular monitoring of blood pressure and heart rate is essential, particularly in individuals at higher risk for cardiovascular complications. This can involve periodic blood pressure checks during follow-up appointments. In some cases, more frequent monitoring, such as home blood pressure monitoring, might be recommended. Routine laboratory tests, particularly for individuals on higher doses or with pre-existing conditions, may be deemed appropriate to monitor for any potential adverse effects. Close collaboration with other healthcare professionals, such as cardiologists or other specialists, might be necessary in certain situations. The goal of monitoring is to ensure both efficacy and safety during stimulant treatment. This continuous assessment, in conjunction with patient feedback, underpins safe and effective management of adult ADHD with stimulant medications.

References

eBNF -ADHD

The Road to Better Sleep: Step-By-Step Guide to Seeking Dental Sleep Medicine Treatment - BRIAN DAVEY DDS INC.   https://drdavey.com/the-road-to-better-sleep-step-by-step-guide-to-seeking-dental-sleep-medicine-treatment/

Normal Adderall Dosage For Adults | Mediserve Apotek. https://mediserveapotek.com/normal-adderall-dosage-for-adults/

13

Non Stimulant Medications for ADHD

While stimulant medications often serve as the first-line treatment for adult ADHD, a significant portion of the population either cannot tolerate them or experiences insufficient symptom relief. For these individuals, nonstimulant medications offer valuable alternative treatment options. These medications work through different mechanisms compared to stimulants, targeting specific neurotransmitter systems involved in ADHD symptomatology. Understanding their distinct actions and potential side effects is crucial for effective clinical decisionmaking.

Atomoxetine, a norepinephrine reuptake inhibitor (NRI), represents a prominent non-stimulant choice. Unlike stimulants that impact both dopamine and norepinephrine, atomoxetine selectively inhibits the reuptake of norepinephrine, leading to increased levels of this neurotransmitter in the synaptic cleft. This enhanced norepinephrine activity contributes to improved attention, focus, and impulse control. The precise mechanisms by which atomoxetine achieves these effects are complex and not fully understood, but its impact on prefrontal cortex function is believed to be significant in its therapeutic action. The prefrontal cortex plays a vital role in executive functions, including planning, working memory, and inhibitory control, all of which are frequently impaired in individuals with ADHD.

The onset of atomoxetine's therapeutic effects is generally slower than that of stimulants. Patients may need several weeks to observe a noticeable improvement in their symptoms. This delayed onset is a key differentiator compared to stimulants, which often provide quicker symptom relief. This slower onset necessitates patient education and careful monitoring during the initial phase of treatment. It's important to manage patient expectations, emphasizing that the full therapeutic benefit may not be evident immediately. Regular follow-up appointments are crucial to assess response and adjust dosage as needed, ensuring optimal symptom management and minimizing potential side effects. The clinician should work collaboratively with the patient to establish realistic goals and timelines for symptom improvement.

Common side effects associated with atomoxetine include decreased appetite, nausea, constipation, and insomnia. These side effects are often dose-related, meaning that reducing the dosage can sometimes alleviate these symptoms. However, it's important to carefully weigh the benefits of symptom reduction against the potential for side effects. In some cases, alternative medications or strategies may be considered if side effects are severe or significantly impact the patient's quality of life. For example, if insomnia is a prominent side effect, administering the medication earlier in the day might help. Dietary changes, such as increased fiber intake, may mitigate constipation. Careful monitoring and open communication between the patient and the clinician are essential for managing potential side effects effectively.

Another class of non-stimulant medications commonly used in ADHD treatment are alpha-2 adrenergic agonists. This class includes guanfacine and clonidine, which act by stimulating alpha-2 adrenergic receptors in the brain. This stimulation reduces norepinephrine release, resulting in a calming effect. While this mechanism might seem counterintuitive given that norepinephrine is involved in attention and focus, the modulation of norepinephrine activity, rather than simply increasing it, can be beneficial in reducing impulsivity and hyperactivity—symptoms that often respond well to this particular mechanism of action. This highlights the complex interplay of neurotransmitters and the multifaceted nature of ADHD itself. The subtle yet significant impact on neural pathways responsible for these symptoms leads to improved focus and behavioral regulation. Unlike atomoxetine, which focuses on reuptake inhibition, these agonists directly influence the release of norepinephrine.

Guanfacine and clonidine are often prescribed for individuals who experience anxiety or emotional dysregulation alongside ADHD symptoms. Their calming effect can be particularly beneficial in these cases, helping manage both the core ADHD symptoms and co-occurring conditions. The use of these medications often necessitates careful titration of the dose to achieve optimal symptom relief while minimizing side effects. Regular monitoring of blood pressure is vital, as both guanfacine and clonidine can lower blood pressure. Patients with pre-existing hypotension should be approached cautiously, with careful consideration of the risks and benefits. Similarly, those with cardiac conditions require careful monitoring and potential adjustment of the medication regimen. These medications often have sedative effects, especially at higher doses. Therefore, starting with a low dose and gradually increasing it while carefully monitoring for side effects is a standard practice.

Side effects of guanfacine and clonidine can include drowsiness, dry mouth, dizziness, and constipation. These side effects, like those associated with atomoxetine, are often dose-related. Adjusting the dosage or altering the time of administration can help manage these issues. The potential for hypotension emphasizes the need for careful monitoring, particularly in patients with pre-existing cardiovascular conditions. Regular blood pressure checks and collaboration with a cardiologist when necessary are essential for ensuring patient safety. Patient education regarding potential side effects and the importance of reporting any concerning symptoms is crucial for effective management.

The choice between atomoxetine and alpha-2 adrenergic agonists depends on several factors, including the patient's individual symptom profile, response to stimulants, and cooccurring conditions. Atomoxetine may be preferred for individuals with predominantly inattentive symptoms, while guanfacine or clonidine might be more suitable for those with prominent hyperactivity, impulsivity, and anxiety. In practice, a combination of non-stimulant medications might be effective for managing a wider range of ADHD symptoms. This often requires careful attention to potential drug interactions. Additionally, the patient's overall health status, including pre-existing medical conditions, plays a significant role in determining the most appropriate treatment strategy.

Beyond atomoxetine, guanfacine, and clonidine, other nonstimulant approaches exist. These may include off-label uses of certain antidepressants or other medications. However, the evidence supporting their efficacy in ADHD specifically is often less robust compared to the established non-stimulants discussed above. The use of these off-label treatments should be considered carefully, with a thorough understanding of potential risks and benefits, and only under the guidance of an experienced clinician knowledgeable in ADHD treatment. These off-label uses usually require close monitoring for both therapeutic efficacy and potential side effects.

The decision regarding non-stimulant medication selection requires a comprehensive assessment of the patient's overall clinical presentation, considering not only ADHD symptoms but also any co-occurring conditions, medical history, and potential drug interactions. This holistic approach ensures that the chosen medication effectively manages ADHD symptoms while minimizing risks. Regular monitoring and open communication between the patient and clinician are critical components of successful treatment with nonstimulant medications for adult ADHD. The goal is not merely to alleviate symptoms but to improve the patient's overall quality of life, functional abilities, and well-being. Therapeutic success depends not only on the medication itself but on the collaborative partnership between the patient and the healthcare provider. This shared decision-making process, characterized by mutual understanding, shared responsibility, and transparent communication, underpins effective and sustainable long-term management of adult ADHD. The journey to managing ADHD symptoms is often a dynamic process requiring adjustments in medication, dosage, or even therapeutic approach as needed. Consistent monitoring, ongoing assessment, and a willingness to adapt treatment plans according to individual patient response are vital for achieving the best possible outcome.

Medication Management and Titration Strategies

The successful management of ADHD with medication hinges not just on selecting the right drug, but on a meticulous approach to titration and ongoing monitoring. This involves a careful process of starting at a low dose, gradually increasing it as needed, and closely observing the patient's response, both positive and negative. The goal is to find the optimal dose—the lowest effective dose that provides symptom relief while minimizing adverse effects. This process requires patience, collaboration, and a willingness to adjust the treatment plan as needed.

Initial dosage selection is guided by several factors, including the patient's age, weight, medical history, and the specific medication chosen. Guidelines often suggest starting with a low dose and gradually increasing it over several weeks, allowing ample time for the medication to reach therapeutic levels and for the patient's body to adjust. This slow titration minimizes the risk of adverse events and allows for a more accurate assessment of the medication's effectiveness. For instance, with stimulant medications like methylphenidate, the initial dose might be significantly lower than the eventual therapeutic dose, with increases occurring in increments of 5-10mg every few days to a couple of weeks, depending on the patient's response and tolerance. This incremental approach allows the clinician to carefully observe for side effects and optimize the therapeutic benefit.

Regular monitoring of treatment response is paramount. This involves frequent communication with the patient to assess the effectiveness of the medication in alleviating ADHD symptoms. Clinicians often utilize standardized rating scales, such as the ADHD Rating Scale-IV (ADHD-RS-IV) or the Conner's Adult ADHD Rating Scales (CAARS), to objectively measure symptom severity before, during, and after medication adjustments. These scales provide a quantifiable measure of improvement, allowing for datadriven decisions regarding medication adjustments. Patients should be encouraged to maintain a daily or weekly log of their symptoms and any side effects experienced. This selfmonitoring empowers the patient and provides valuable data for the clinician. This collaborative approach ensures that the treatment plan remains responsive to the patient's evolving needs.

Side effects are a common occurrence with ADHD medications, and their management is an integral part of successful medication management. Stimulant medications, for example, can cause insomnia, decreased appetite, anxiety, and increased blood pressure and heart rate. Nonstimulant medications have their own unique profiles of side effects, which may include nausea, drowsiness, dizziness, and changes in blood pressure or heart rate. Careful attention to these potential side effects is necessary during the titration process. A detailed discussion of the potential side effects should occur prior to starting medication.

Strategies for managing side effects vary depending on the specific side effect and the medication used. For instance, insomnia associated with stimulants can be managed by adjusting the timing of medication administration (taking it earlier in the day) or using a lower dose in the evening. Decreased appetite may require adjustments to the patient's diet, possibly incorporating smaller, more frequent meals that are nutritionally dense. If anxiety is a significant concern, the clinician may consider lowering the dose or switching to an alternative medication with a more favorable side effect profile. Sometimes, a combination of medication and behavioral strategies may be necessary to manage specific side effects effectively. For example, relaxation techniques or cognitive behavioral therapy (CBT) might be used to address anxiety or insomnia alongside medication adjustments.

The use of objective measures is crucial for guiding titration decisions. In addition to rating scales, clinicians may monitor vital signs like blood pressure and heart rate, particularly with stimulant medications, to identify any potential cardiovascular effects. Laboratory tests may be necessary to monitor for potential metabolic side effects or to assess the impact on other organ systems. The decision to increase the dose, decrease the dose, or even switch medications should be data-driven. Blindly increasing the dosage without careful monitoring can lead to unnecessary side effects, while not increasing the dosage sufficiently may mean the medication isn't effective. Therefore, this is a process of thoughtful adjustments, guided by observation, feedback and ongoing assessment of the effectiveness of treatment.

Another crucial aspect of medication management is addressing potential drug interactions. Patients often take other medications, either for ADHD comorbidities or for other medical conditions. It's imperative to carefully review the patient's medication history to identify any potential interactions that could affect the efficacy or safety of ADHD medications. For example, some medications can increase the metabolism of stimulants, leading to reduced efficacy. Conversely, some medications may interact with nonstimulant medications, leading to an increased risk of side effects. Therefore a careful review of the patient's complete medication regimen, including over-the-counter medications and herbal supplements, is vital to minimizing potential interactions and ensuring medication safety.

Patient education plays a crucial role in successful medication management. Patients need to understand the purpose of the medication, its potential benefits and side effects, the importance of adherence, and how to monitor their response to the medication. This involves open communication with the clinician, sharing any concerns or challenges they encounter. The clinician should empower the patient to actively participate in the treatment process, encouraging them to track their symptoms, report any side effects, and ask questions. This shared decision-making approach ensures that the patient feels heard and understood, enhancing their adherence to the treatment plan and improving overall treatment outcomes.

Finally, recognizing that medication management is a dynamic process is essential. What works initially may not continue to be effective over time. Lifestyle changes, stress levels, and the natural course of the condition can influence the efficacy of medication. Therefore, regular follow-up appointments are crucial for monitoring treatment response, adjusting the medication as needed, and addressing any emerging issues. This ongoing assessment allows for timely interventions to maintain optimal symptom control and prevent relapses. The collaborative relationship between the patient and the clinician is the cornerstone of successful long-term medication management for adult ADHD. This dynamic partnership, built on open communication, shared decision-making, and a mutual commitment to achieving the best possible outcome, forms the basis of a successful treatment journey. Flexibility, ongoing monitoring, and responsiveness to the individual patient's needs remain at the heart of successful pharmacologic intervention for adult ADHD.

References

eBNF -ADHD

Clark, K. L. (2017). Evaluation of Depression Screening Practices in Comorbid Patients in the Primary Care Setting. https://core.ac.uk/download/232591109.pdf

14

Addressing Common Side Effects of ADHD Medications

Building upon the careful titration and ongoing monitoring discussed previously, we now turn to a crucial aspect of pharmacological ADHD treatment: managing the side effects. While medication can significantly improve symptoms, it's important to understand that these medications, both stimulants and non-stimulants, can cause various side effects. These side effects vary in severity and frequency, depending on the individual, the specific medication, and the dosage. Open communication between the patient and their prescribing physician is paramount in effectively managing these side effects and ensuring the continued efficacy and tolerability of the treatment. The goal is not to avoid all side effects—that's often unrealistic—but to minimize those that significantly impact the patient's quality of life and to develop strategies to mitigate their impact.

One of the most frequently reported side effects of stimulant medications like methylphenidate (Ritalin, Concerta) and amphetamine (Adderall, Vyvanse) is decreased appetite. This can lead to weight loss, particularly concerning in individuals already struggling with maintaining a healthy weight. Strategies to counteract this include: scheduling medication doses strategically, e.g., taking them after meals rather than before; consuming calorie-dense, nutrient-rich snacks throughout the day; and working with a registered dietitian to develop a meal plan that ensures adequate caloric intake and nutritional balance. It's important to remember that weight loss is a significant concern, not just for overall health but also because it can impact medication efficacy and potentially necessitate dose adjustments.

Insomnia is another common side effect of stimulant medications. The stimulating effect can interfere with the ability to fall asleep and maintain sleep throughout the night. This necessitates a careful consideration of the timing of medication administration. The last dose should ideally be taken several hours before bedtime. In some cases, a long acting formulation might be considered to reduce the frequency of dosing and minimize the evening impact on sleep. Furthermore, good sleep hygiene is critical. This includes establishing a regular sleep schedule, creating a relaxing bedtime routine, ensuring a dark, quiet, and cool sleep environment, and avoiding caffeine and alcohol before bed. If insomnia persists despite these measures, the prescribing physician may consider adjusting the dose or medication type or adding a sleep aid, such as melatonin, under their guidance.

Other gastrointestinal side effects such as nausea, stomach upset, and constipation are also relatively common. These can often be mitigated by taking the medication with food or adjusting the medication schedule. For example, taking the medication with a full meal can help reduce nausea. Increasing water intake and incorporating fiber-rich foods into the diet can help alleviate constipation. If these issues persist, it's important to consult with the physician who may consider a dose adjustment or suggest an alternative medication. In severe cases, over-the-counter medications for nausea or constipation may be appropriate, but always under medical supervision.

Cardiovascular side effects, while relatively rare, are an important consideration, particularly with stimulant medications. These can include increased heart rate and blood pressure. Regular monitoring of blood pressure and heart rate is crucial, particularly at the start of medication and during dose adjustments. Individuals with pre-existing cardiovascular conditions should be monitored closely. In some cases, alternative medications may be considered, and any concerns should be immediately addressed with the prescribing physician. The physician will balance the benefits of ADHD medication against the potential risks based on the patient's specific circumstances.

Central nervous system side effects, such as anxiety, nervousness, headache, and dizziness, can also occur with stimulant medications. These side effects can be dose related, meaning they are more likely to occur at higher doses. Reducing the dose, or switching to a lower-potency formulation, might mitigate these issues. In some cases, other strategies might be helpful, such as regular exercise, stress management techniques, and sufficient hydration. Again, open communication with the prescribing physician is vital in managing these concerns. They can help determine if the benefit of the medication outweighs these side effects and can suggest alternative treatment strategies if necessary.

Non-stimulant medications, such as atomoxetine (Strattera) and alpha-2 agonists like guanfacine (Intuniv) and clonidine (Kapvay), generally have a different side effect profile. While they are often better tolerated than stimulants, they can still cause side effects. Atomoxetine, for example, can cause nausea, constipation, decreased appetite, and insomnia, though often to a lesser degree than stimulants. Alpha-2 agonists, on the other hand, can lead to drowsiness, dizziness, low blood pressure (hypotension), and fatigue. These side effects often diminish with time as the body adjusts to the medication. However, if they are persistent or severe, dose adjustment or medication changes might be necessary.

Managing side effects effectively requires a collaborative approach. Patients should actively participate in their treatment by reporting all side effects to their physicians, promptly and accurately. Keeping a medication diary can be a valuable tool for both patients and clinicians, documenting not just the medication taken but also any observed side effects, their severity, and the timing of their onset. This detailed record facilitates a more informed discussion with the physician, allowing them to assess the situation and adjust the treatment plan accordingly. The diary can also include other pertinent information such as sleep quality, appetite, mood changes, and overall functioning, providing a more complete picture of the patient's response to the medication.

For example, if a patient experiences significant insomnia after taking their medication, documenting the time of medication administration, the onset of sleep problems, and any other relevant details can assist the physician in determining whether a dose adjustment or a change in medication timing is necessary. Similarly, recording changes in appetite can help monitor potential weight loss and guide decisions on dietary adjustments or medication modifications. This active participation enhances the effectiveness of the therapeutic process, leading to better management of ADHD symptoms and improved quality of life.

The importance of regular follow-up appointments cannot be overstated. These appointments provide opportunities for physicians to monitor the effectiveness of the medication, assess for any emerging side effects, and make necessary adjustments to the treatment plan. The collaborative relationship fostered during these visits allows for open communication, shared decision-making, and a mutual understanding of the patient's needs and goals. This ongoing assessment is crucial for ensuring the long-term success of pharmacological interventions for adult ADHD.

Finally, it is crucial to remember that medication is just one component of a holistic approach to managing ADHD. Lifestyle modifications, including regular exercise, a healthy diet, sufficient sleep, and stress management techniques, can significantly contribute to symptom control and overall wellbeing. These lifestyle changes can work synergistically with medication to enhance its effectiveness and minimize the impact of any potential side effects. A comprehensive treatment plan that incorporates both pharmacological and non-pharmacological interventions often leads to the best possible outcomes for individuals with adult ADHD.

Through careful monitoring, open communication, and a collaborative approach, the side effects of medication can be effectively managed, enabling individuals to experience the full benefits of treatment while maintaining a high quality of life.

References

Alcohol's Harm on Athletic Performance and Recovery. https://www.conquermovementpt.com/conquer-movement-blog/athletesbane-0

Fatigue – MNetwork. https://www.mnetwork.org.uk/resources/fatigue/

Subtle Cocaine Addiction Symptoms You May be Missing. https://cocainerehabcenter.com/cocaine-addiction/subtle-cocaine-addiction-symptoms-may-missing/

Empowering Holistic Mental Health Therapy at Schoen Clinic Chelsea. https://www.schoen-clinic.co.uk/post/what-are-the-advantages-of-holistic-mental-health-therapy

Alcohol's Harm on Athletic Performance and Recovery. https://www.conquermovementpt.com/conquer-movement-blog/athletesbane-0

Depression Signs, Symptoms, and Support -. https://newconnectionspsychology.com.au/blog/depression-signs-symptoms-and-support/

ADHD in Adults: Symptoms Checklist. https://memorial2u.com/adult-adhd-symptoms-checklist-recognizing-signs.html

15

Monitoring Treatment Response and Medication Adjustments

Following the initial prescription and the management of potential side effects, the ongoing process of monitoring treatment response and making necessary adjustments is critical for successful ADHD management. This is not a static process; it requires regular assessment and a willingness to adapt the treatment plan based on the individual's progress and experiences. The goal is to achieve optimal symptom control with minimal side effects, a balance that requires careful observation and communication between the patient and their healthcare provider.

The initial assessment, typically conducted within a few weeks of starting medication, focuses on evaluating the impact of the medication on core ADHD symptoms. This involves a multifaceted approach, incorporating various tools and perspectives. The patient's self-report is crucial. They may use rating scales, such as the ADHD Rating Scale-IV (ADHD-RS-IV) or the Adult ADHD Self-Report Scale (ASRS), to quantify their experience of symptoms like inattention, hyperactivity, and impulsivity. These scales provide a structured way to track changes in symptom severity over time. These self-reported data, while valuable, should be complemented with information from other sources. For example, a spouse, partner, family member, or close friend can provide collateral information, offering a different perspective on the patient's behavior and symptom presentation. Their observations can help identify areas where improvement is evident and areas where adjustments might be necessary.

The clinician will also conduct clinical interviews to explore the patient's subjective experience. This is not just about numerical scores; it's about gaining a nuanced understanding of how the medication affects their daily life—their work performance, their relationships, their ability to manage tasks, their overall mood and emotional regulation. This qualitative data enriches the quantitative data from rating scales, offering a more complete picture of the treatment's impact. Furthermore, the clinician assesses the presence and severity of any side effects, noting their impact on the patient's daily functioning.

Depending on the patient's response and the presence of side effects, adjustments to the medication regimen might be necessary. These adjustments can involve several strategies. Dose titration is often the first approach. If the initial dose proves insufficient to control symptoms, the clinician might gradually increase the dose until an optimal balance between symptom relief and side effects is reached. This titration process is typically slow and incremental, with close monitoring at each dosage level to observe both the therapeutic effects and any emerging side effects. Conversely, if side effects are significantly impacting the patient's quality of life, a dose reduction might be warranted. The goal is to find the lowest effective dose that provides adequate symptom relief.

In cases where the initial medication choice proves ineffective, a switch to a different medication may be considered. This might involve transitioning from a stimulant to a non-stimulant, or vice versa, or exploring different medications within the same class. For example, if methylphenidate isn't well-tolerated, the clinician might consider amphetamine-based medication, or if a stimulant proves ineffective, a non-stimulant such as atomoxetine might be tried. The choice of medication will depend on various factors, including the patient's individual response, the presence of comorbidities, potential drug interactions, and personal preferences. It's crucial to emphasize that switching medications isn't a sign of failure, but rather a reflection of the personalized nature of ADHD treatment.

Regular follow-up appointments are essential throughout the treatment process. These appointments provide opportunities to monitor the effectiveness of the medication, assess for side effects, discuss any challenges the patient is facing, and make necessary adjustments to the treatment plan. The frequency of these appointments will depend on the individual's needs and progress. In the initial phase, more frequent visits might be necessary, perhaps every one to two weeks, while later on, appointments may become less frequent, perhaps every few months, as long as the treatment is effective and well-tolerated.

Beyond medication adjustments, a crucial aspect of monitoring treatment response involves addressing the potential interaction between medication and other aspects of the patient's life. For instance, medication effectiveness can be influenced by lifestyle factors such as sleep, diet, and exercise. Insufficient sleep can exacerbate ADHD symptoms and reduce medication effectiveness. A poor diet can similarly affect mood and energy levels, potentially negating the benefits of the medication. Regular exercise, on the other hand, can have a positive synergistic effect, improving mood, reducing stress, and potentially enhancing the impact of medication.

The role of comorbid conditions also needs consideration. Many individuals with ADHD also experience other mental health conditions, such as anxiety, depression, or obsessivecompulsive disorder. These conditions can complicate ADHD treatment and may require separate management strategies. The interplay between ADHD medication and these comorbid conditions needs careful consideration to prevent adverse effects or medication interactions. For example, certain ADHD medications might interact with antidepressants or other psychiatric medications. A thorough understanding of the patient's complete medical history, including any other conditions or medications they are taking, is therefore crucial for making informed decisions about ADHD treatment.

It is important to underscore that the monitoring process is a collaborative effort involving both the patient and the healthcare provider. Open communication between them is vital. Patients should actively participate in their treatment, honestly reporting their experiences, both positive and negative, regarding the medication's effects and any side effects. They should not hesitate to raise concerns or ask questions. A patient's active participation significantly improves the chances of finding an effective and welltolerated treatment regimen.

Moreover, adherence to the medication regimen is crucial for successful treatment. Missing doses or inconsistent medication use can reduce the effectiveness of the medication and make it challenging to assess the true impact of the treatment. Strategies to improve adherence might include setting reminders, using pill organizers, and establishing a daily routine that incorporates medication intake. The healthcare provider can offer support and guidance in developing strategies to enhance medication adherence.

Finally, the concept of treatment success needs careful consideration. It isn't simply about achieving a complete absence of symptoms; it's about improving functional outcomes. Successful treatment aims to enhance the individual's quality of life, enabling them to function more effectively in various areas, such as work, relationships, and daily living activities. The assessment of treatment success should, therefore, encompass a broad range of outcomes, including subjective improvements in mood and well-being, objective improvements in work productivity or academic performance, and improved interpersonal relationships. Regularly monitoring these aspects is essential to ensure that the treatment plan is truly achieving its desired goals and making a meaningful positive impact on the patient's life. The journey of managing ADHD is a continuous process, and consistent monitoring, open communication, and a collaborative approach are key elements of long-term success. The flexible and adaptive nature of treatment ensures that individuals can find the best path towards improved functionality and overall well-being, tailored to their unique circumstances and needs.

References

Causes of RLS (Restless Legs Syndrome) - Truffles Vein Specialists. https://hopecenterknox.org/sl-262175/causes-of-rls-restless-legs-syndrome

Normal Adderall Dosage For Adults | Mediserve Apotek. https://mediserveapotek.com/normal-adderall-dosage-for-adults/

16

Behavioral Therapy and Cognitive Behavioral Therapy CBT

Behavioral therapy and Cognitive Behavioral Therapy (CBT) represent powerful non-pharmacological approaches to managing the multifaceted challenges of adult ADHD. These therapies work by targeting specific cognitive and behavioral patterns associated with the condition, helping individuals develop compensatory strategies and improve their overall functioning. Unlike medication, which primarily affects neurochemical processes, behavioral and CBT interventions equip individuals with the tools and techniques to actively manage their symptoms and improve their quality of life.

Behavioral therapy focuses on modifying observable behaviors through techniques like reinforcement and punishment. In the context of ADHD, this translates to strategies that reward desired behaviors, such as focused attention and task completion, and minimize behaviors that hinder success, such as impulsivity and procrastination. A common technique is behavioral activation, where individuals are encouraged to engage in activities that are rewarding and contribute to a sense of accomplishment. This can be particularly helpful for adults with ADHD who often experience low motivation and difficulty initiating tasks. For example, a person struggling with procrastination in their work might be guided to break down large projects into smaller, more manageable steps, rewarding themselves for each completed step. This incremental approach fosters a sense of progress and reduces the overwhelming feeling often associated with larger undertakings. The therapist works collaboratively with the individual to identify specific target behaviors, create a system for monitoring progress, and develop individualized reinforcement strategies. This could involve setting daily or weekly goals, using reward charts or point systems, and implementing consequences for non-compliance.

Cognitive Behavioral Therapy (CBT), on the other hand, goes beyond behavior modification by exploring the interplay between thoughts, feelings, and behaviors. Individuals with ADHD often experience negative self-talk, which can exacerbate symptoms. CBT helps individuals identify and challenge these negative thought patterns, replacing them with more realistic and adaptive ones. For instance, someone who constantly criticizes themselves for making mistakes might learn to reframe their self-criticism, acknowledging the mistake but focusing on learning from it rather than dwelling on self-blame. This process involves identifying cognitive distortions, such as all-or-nothing thinking, overgeneralization, and catastrophizing, which are common in individuals with ADHD. The therapist helps the individual develop strategies to challenge these distortions and develop more balanced and rational perspectives.

A key component of CBT for ADHD is the development of self-monitoring skills. Individuals are taught to track their thoughts, feelings, and behaviors over time, gaining insight into patterns and triggers that contribute to their symptoms. This self-awareness enables them to anticipate challenges and develop proactive strategies to manage them. For example, an individual might realize that they are more prone to impulsivity when they are tired or stressed. This awareness allows them to implement coping mechanisms, such as taking a break, engaging in relaxation techniques, or seeking support when needed.

A significant aspect of CBT for ADHD involves teaching time management and organizational skills. Many individuals with ADHD struggle with planning, prioritizing, and completing tasks efficiently. CBT can help develop strategies such as breaking down tasks into smaller steps, using visual aids like checklists and calendars, and employing time management techniques like the Pomodoro Technique (working in focused intervals with short breaks). This structured approach can significantly improve productivity and reduce feelings of overwhelm. Furthermore, CBT can address the challenges associated with executive dysfunction, a core feature of ADHD. Executive functions, such as working memory, planning, and inhibitory control, are often impaired in individuals with ADHD. CBT helps individuals develop compensatory strategies to mitigate these impairments, such as using external memory aids, developing structured routines, and practicing mindfulness techniques to improve attention and focus.

The integration of behavioral techniques and CBT principles is often highly effective. For example, a therapist might combine behavioral activation with cognitive restructuring to help an individual overcome procrastination. Behavioral activation would encourage the individual to engage in productive activities, while cognitive restructuring would help them challenge negative thoughts that contribute to procrastination, such as "I'll never finish this," or "I'm not good enough." This integrated approach targets both the behavioral and cognitive aspects of the challenge, promoting sustained change.

The success of behavioral and CBT interventions relies heavily on the collaborative relationship between the therapist and the individual. The therapist acts as a guide and coach, empowering the individual to take an active role in their treatment. This partnership ensures that the interventions are tailored to the individual's specific needs and preferences. Regular sessions provide an opportunity to discuss progress, adjust strategies, and address any challenges encountered. The therapist provides feedback, encouragement, and support, fostering self-efficacy and promoting long-term adherence to treatment plans.

Furthermore, homework assignments are an integral part of both behavioral therapy and CBT. These assignments provide opportunities for individuals to practice the skills and techniques learned during therapy sessions in their everyday lives. This practice reinforces learning and promotes generalization of skills to various contexts. For instance, an individual might be asked to practice mindfulness exercises daily, track their mood and energy levels, or use a planner to schedule tasks. Regular feedback on homework assignments allows the therapist to monitor progress and make necessary adjustments to the treatment plan.

The duration of behavioral and CBT treatment for ADHD varies depending on individual needs and treatment goals. Typically, treatment involves weekly sessions for several months, or even longer in some cases. The focus is on developing sustainable coping strategies and fostering selfmanagement skills that can be utilized long-term. Follow-up sessions may be recommended to monitor progress and provide ongoing support. While there is no one-size-fits-all approach, the integration of behavioral and CBT techniques represents a valuable non-pharmacological avenue for managing the challenges associated with ADHD, offering individuals the tools and skills they need to lead fulfilling and productive lives.

Beyond the core techniques already mentioned, specific strategies within behavioral therapy and CBT can be tailored to address various ADHD symptoms. For instance, impulse control can be improved through techniques like selfinstruction training, where individuals learn to give themselves verbal cues and reminders before acting impulsively. This technique encourages pause and reflection before responding, preventing impulsive reactions. Similarly, attention deficits can be addressed through attention training exercises, such as focusing on a specific visual stimulus for extended periods, gradually increasing the duration and difficulty of the task. These exercises help improve sustained attention and concentration, critical skills for managing everyday life challenges.

Organizational skills are equally important for individuals with ADHD, and CBT can play a vital role in improving this area. Techniques such as externalizing memory systems (using calendars, to-do lists, and reminder apps) or employing time-blocking strategies (allocating specific time slots for particular tasks) can significantly improve organization and productivity. These methods reduce reliance on memory and promote a more structured approach to task management.

Moreover, the therapeutic relationship itself plays a crucial role in the success of these interventions. A strong therapeutic alliance, characterized by mutual trust, respect, and collaboration, is essential for fostering motivation and engagement in treatment. The therapist's empathy, understanding, and patience are critical in helping individuals navigate the emotional challenges associated with ADHD. Regularly reviewing progress and adjusting the treatment plan based on the individual's feedback enhances the likelihood of achieving positive outcomes.

Finally, the generalization of skills learned in therapy is a crucial factor for long-term success. The goal is not simply to improve functioning in the therapy room, but to equip individuals with skills they can apply effectively across various life domains, including work, relationships, and leisure activities. This requires consistent effort and practice outside of therapy sessions, emphasizing the importance of integrating the techniques learned into daily routines. Regular follow-up sessions can provide valuable support and guidance in this process, ensuring lasting improvements in symptom management and overall quality of life. By incorporating these multifaceted behavioral and CBT strategies, individuals with ADHD can gain a sense of mastery over their symptoms, leading to improved selfesteem, increased independence, and greater overall wellbeing.

References

10 Things You Learned In Kindergarden That Will Help You Get Diagnose ADHD - worldhealthstock. https://worldhealthstock.com/10-things-you-learned-in-kindergarden-that-will-help-you-get-diagnose-adhd/

What is Interpersonal reconstructive therapy? – LIBERTY PSYCHOLOGICAL ASSOCIATION. https://shervanshahhian.com/2023/05/10/what-is-interpersonal-reconstructive-therapy/

Simmons, S., French, W., Boydston, L., & Varley, C. (2022). Obsessive compulsive disorder. Journal of Alternative Medicine Research, 14(3), 277-286.

CBT | Counseling & Wellness Collective. https://www.counselingandwellnessco.com/cognitive-behavioral-therapy

Cognitive Behavioural Therapy (CBT) | APT USA. https://www.aptmentalhealthtraining.com/cognitive-behavioral-therapy.html

Managing ADHD in College | Macaroni KID Richmond. https://richmond.macaronikid.com/articles/6438293736b421177cc956ee/managing-adhd-in-college

Connecting the Dots Object Permanence in ADHD Explained – Gitar Kursları. https://gitarkurslari.com.tr/connecting-the-dots-object-permanence-in-adhd-explained/

The Role of Therapy for Depression | Elevate Psychiatry. https://elevatepsychiatry.com/blog/the-role-of-therapy-in-managing-and-overcoming-depression/

Unlocking Minds: How Cognitive-Behavioral Therapy Transforms Lives. https://mindfulharmonyoasis.com/how-does-cognitive-behavioral-therapy-work/

CBT (Cognitive Behavioural Therapy) Milton Keynes - Birch Barn Therapies. https://birchbarntherapies.co.uk/treatments/cbt-cognitive-behavioural-therapy/

50 Interview Questions For Therapist (With Answers). https://huntr.co/interview-questions/therapist

17

Lifestyle Modifications for ADHD Management

Building upon the foundational strategies of behavioral and cognitive behavioral therapies, we now turn our attention to the crucial role of lifestyle modifications in managing adult ADHD. While medication and therapy address the core neurobiological and cognitive aspects of the condition, lifestyle changes act as powerful complements, enhancing the effectiveness of other interventions and contributing significantly to overall well-being. These modifications are not merely add-ons; they represent essential components of a comprehensive and holistic approach to ADHD management. Think of them as the scaffolding that supports the structure built by therapy and medication, providing a stable and resilient framework for long-term success.

Let's begin with the often-overlooked, yet critically important, area of sleep hygiene. Insufficient sleep, or poor sleep quality, exacerbates virtually every ADHD symptom. The hyperactivity, impulsivity, and inattention already present can become dramatically amplified when sleep deprivation is a factor. The impact extends beyond the immediate experience of fatigue; it interferes with cognitive function, emotional regulation, and executive functioning, making it harder to focus, plan, organize, and resist impulsive behaviors. Improving sleep hygiene isn't just about getting more hours; it's about optimizing the quality of those hours. This requires a multi-pronged approach.

First, establish a consistent sleep schedule, going to bed and waking up at roughly the same time each day, even on weekends. This helps regulate your body's natural sleepwake cycle, making it easier to fall asleep and wake up feeling refreshed. Second, create a relaxing bedtime routine.

This could include a warm bath, reading a book, listening to calming music, or practicing relaxation techniques like deep breathing or meditation. Avoid screen time at least an hour before bed, as the blue light emitted from electronic devices can interfere with melatonin production, a hormone crucial for regulating sleep. Third, ensure your sleep environment is conducive to rest. This means creating a dark, quiet, and cool room, free from distractions. Consider using earplugs or an eye mask if necessary. Finally, address any underlying medical conditions or sleep disorders that may be contributing to sleep problems. If you consistently struggle with sleep, consult a healthcare professional to rule out any underlying medical issues and explore potential solutions. Remember, improving sleep isn't a one-time fix; it requires consistent effort and attention to detail.

Diet plays another significant role in ADHD management. While there's no single "ADHD diet," research suggests that certain dietary changes can positively influence symptoms. Focusing on a balanced diet rich in fruits, vegetables, whole grains, and lean protein provides the body with the essential nutrients needed for optimal brain function. Limiting processed foods, sugary drinks, and excessive caffeine is equally important. These items can lead to energy crashes, mood swings, and increased impulsivity, directly counteracting the goals of ADHD management. Consider keeping a food diary to track your eating habits and identify potential triggers for negative symptoms. Pay attention to how different foods affect your energy levels, focus, and mood. This self-monitoring can provide valuable insights into the connection between diet and ADHD symptoms.

Furthermore, consulting a registered dietitian or nutritionist can provide personalized guidance on creating a balanced diet tailored to your specific needs and preferences.

Regular physical exercise is another powerful tool in the ADHD management arsenal. Exercise isn't just about physical health; it significantly impacts mental well-being, contributing to improved mood, focus, and cognitive function. Aerobic exercise, such as running, swimming, or cycling, has been shown to be particularly effective in improving attention and reducing hyperactivity. However, any form of physical activity, from brisk walking to team sports, can be beneficial. The key is to find activities you enjoy and can stick with consistently. Aim for at least 30 minutes of moderate-intensity exercise most days of the week. Remember, the benefits of exercise are cumulative. The more consistently you engage in physical activity, the greater the positive impact on your ADHD symptoms. Moreover, consider incorporating mindfulness-based movement practices like yoga or tai chi. These practices combine physical activity with mindfulness techniques, promoting both physical and mental well-being. The focus on the present moment during these activities can help improve attention and reduce stress, contributing to better overall symptom management.

Stress management is undeniably crucial. Individuals with ADHD are often more susceptible to the negative effects of stress, and chronic stress can significantly worsen ADHD symptoms. Developing effective stress management techniques is therefore essential. Techniques range from simple relaxation exercises like deep breathing and progressive muscle relaxation to more complex approaches like mindfulness meditation and cognitive restructuring. Deep breathing, for instance, can be practiced anywhere, anytime, providing a quick and effective way to calm the nervous system. Progressive muscle relaxation involves systematically tensing and releasing different muscle groups, helping to reduce physical tension associated with stress. Mindfulness meditation cultivates awareness of the present moment, helping to reduce rumination and worry, common features in individuals with ADHD. Cognitive restructuring involves identifying and challenging negative or unhelpful thought patterns, replacing them with more balanced and realistic perspectives. Learning to recognize stress triggers and developing coping mechanisms specific to those triggers is also essential. This may involve adjusting work schedules, delegating tasks, or seeking social support. Stress management is an ongoing process, requiring continuous effort and adaptation. It's not a one-size-fits-all solution, and experimentation may be needed to find the techniques that work best for you.

Beyond these core areas, other lifestyle modifications can contribute to better ADHD management. These include optimizing your work environment to minimize distractions, using organizational tools and techniques, prioritizing tasks effectively, and breaking down large tasks into smaller, more manageable steps. Creating a structured daily routine can provide a sense of order and predictability, reducing the potential for overwhelm. Utilizing visual aids, reminders, and checklists can enhance organization and reduce reliance on memory, a common challenge for individuals with ADHD. Furthermore, cultivating strong social connections and supportive relationships can provide a crucial buffer against the challenges of ADHD, offering emotional support and practical assistance. Regular social interaction can also combat feelings of isolation and improve overall mood.

In conclusion, lifestyle modifications are not a replacement for medication or therapy but rather essential complements. By focusing on sleep hygiene, diet, exercise, stress management, and other related strategies, individuals with ADHD can significantly enhance their ability to manage symptoms and improve their overall quality of life. These modifications represent proactive steps towards self-care, empowering individuals to take control of their well-being and build a more fulfilling life. The integration of these strategies with other treatment modalities represents a holistic approach to ADHD management, maximizing the likelihood of sustained improvement and long-term success. Remember, consistent effort and perseverance are key to reaping the full benefits of these lifestyle changes. They are a journey, not a destination, requiring ongoing commitment and self-compassion. Don't hesitate to seek support from healthcare professionals or support groups along the way; the journey is often smoother and more successful when shared.

References

(2023). HOW CAN I BOOST MY Immune System Through My Gut. Alternative Medicine, (70), 26-29.

Pearson, K. E. (2017). Effects of Anxiety Treatment Using Coping Cat on Problem Behaviors in the Classroom. https://core.ac.uk/download/234047741.pdf

18

Mindfulness and Meditation Techniques for ADHD

Mindfulness and meditation, practices often associated with relaxation and stress reduction, offer a unique and powerful approach to managing the core symptoms of adult ADHD. These techniques, rooted in ancient traditions but increasingly supported by modern neuroscience, work by cultivating present moment awareness and enhancing self regulation, directly addressing the challenges of inattention, hyperactivity, and impulsivity. Unlike medications that primarily target neurochemical imbalances, mindfulness and meditation directly train the brain to improve its capacity for focused attention and emotional control.

The core principle underlying these practices is the cultivation of non-judgmental awareness. Instead of battling racing thoughts or struggling against feelings of restlessness, the individual learns to observe these experiences without reacting or getting swept away. This seemingly simple shift in perspective can have a profound impact on ADHD symptoms. For example, the constant stream of distracting thoughts that characterize ADHD can be seen not as a personal failing, but simply as mental events unfolding in the present moment. By observing these thoughts without engaging with them, the individual gains a sense of distance and control, reducing their power to derail attention and disrupt focus.

One of the most accessible mindfulness techniques for individuals with ADHD is mindful breathing. This involves focusing on the sensation of the breath as it enters and leaves the body, noticing the rise and fall of the chest or abdomen. When the mind wanders—and it inevitably will—the practice isn't to chastise oneself but gently redirect attention back to the breath. This simple act of repeatedly returning to the present moment strengthens the brain's ability to sustain attention, a core deficit in ADHD. Regular practice, even for just a few minutes each day, can improve focus and concentration over time.

Mindful body scans are another helpful tool. This involves systematically bringing awareness to different parts of the body, noticing sensations without judgment. This practice can be incredibly grounding, particularly for individuals who experience restlessness and hyperactivity. By shifting attention to the physical body, the mind is less likely to be pulled into the whirlwind of thoughts and worries that often characterize ADHD. This heightened body awareness can also improve proprioception—the sense of where one's body is in space—which can be beneficial for individuals with motor impulsivity.

Meditation techniques build upon the foundations of mindfulness. While mindfulness is about present moment awareness, meditation often involves a more structured practice, incorporating specific techniques to cultivate attention and calm the mind. There are numerous forms of meditation, and finding the right approach is crucial.

Some individuals with ADHD might find guided meditations particularly helpful, as the voice of the guide provides a focal point and a sense of structure. Others might prefer silent meditation, focusing on the breath or a mantra. Experimentation is key; what works for one person may not work for another.

Mindfulness-based cognitive therapy (MBCT) is a structured program that integrates mindfulness practices with cognitive behavioral therapy (CBT) techniques. It is particularly useful for individuals with ADHD who struggle with emotional regulation and negative thought patterns. MBCT teaches individuals to observe their thoughts and emotions without judgment, and to identify and challenge negative automatic thoughts that contribute to emotional distress. By combining mindfulness with cognitive restructuring, MBCT aims to break the cycle of negative thoughts and feelings, improving emotional well-being and reducing reactivity.

Transcendental Meditation (TM) is another technique gaining traction in the ADHD community. TM involves the silent repetition of a personalized mantra, a word or sound chosen specifically for the individual. Regular TM practice can promote relaxation, reduce stress, and improve focus. Studies have shown that TM may reduce symptoms of ADHD, particularly inattention and hyperactivity. However, it's important to note that the effectiveness of TM, like other meditation techniques, can vary among individuals.

The benefits of mindfulness and meditation for adult ADHD extend beyond symptom management. These practices can foster self-compassion, a crucial element in managing the chronic challenges associated with ADHD. Individuals with ADHD often struggle with self-criticism and feelings of inadequacy. Mindfulness practices help cultivate selfacceptance and self-understanding, allowing individuals to treat themselves with kindness and patience. This shift in perspective can be transformative, reducing feelings of frustration and self-doubt.

To integrate mindfulness and meditation effectively into daily life, it is essential to establish a consistent practice. Start with short sessions, perhaps just 5-10 minutes a day, and gradually increase the duration as comfort and skill develop. Consistency is key to reaping the full benefits. It's also helpful to find a quiet, comfortable space where you can practice without distractions. Consider using a meditation app or guided meditation recordings, especially in the early stages of practice. Many free and paid apps offer a wide variety of guided meditations, catering to different experience levels and preferences.

While the scientific evidence supporting the effectiveness of mindfulness and meditation for ADHD is still evolving, a growing body of research suggests these techniques offer significant potential benefits. Studies have shown that mindfulness interventions can improve attention, reduce impulsivity, and enhance emotional regulation in individuals with ADHD. Moreover, the non-pharmacological nature of these practices makes them a valuable complement to medication and therapy, offering a holistic approach to managing the multifaceted challenges of ADHD. However, it's crucial to remember that mindfulness and meditation are not quick fixes. They require consistent practice and patience to yield tangible benefits.

It's crucial to approach mindfulness and meditation with realistic expectations. It's not about completely silencing the mind or achieving a state of perpetual calm; rather, it's about learning to observe thoughts and feelings without judgment and to cultivate a more accepting relationship with oneself. Individuals may experience initial frustration as they grapple with the challenge of focusing attention and quieting the mind. This is normal and should not be seen as a sign of failure. Perseverance and self-compassion are key to success.

Integrating mindfulness practices into daily life extends beyond formal meditation sessions. Moments of mindful awareness can be cultivated throughout the day, such as paying close attention to the sensations of eating a meal, engaging fully in a conversation, or appreciating the beauty of nature. These small acts of mindfulness can help to cultivate a greater sense of presence and focus, reducing the impact of ADHD symptoms on daily functioning. Even seemingly mundane tasks, like washing dishes or walking the dog, can become opportunities for mindful practice.

The benefits of mindfulness and meditation are not limited to the direct improvement of ADHD symptoms. These practices can also enhance overall well-being, reducing stress, anxiety, and depression, which often co-occur with ADHD. By promoting emotional regulation and selfawareness, mindfulness and meditation can improve relationships, increase productivity, and enhance overall quality of life. This holistic approach to well-being is crucial in managing a condition as multifaceted as ADHD.

Ultimately, the journey of integrating mindfulness and meditation into ADHD management is a personal one. What works for one individual may not work for another. Experimentation with different techniques, finding a supportive community, and seeking guidance from experienced professionals can all be essential components of this process. The key is to find a practice that resonates with the individual, fostering a sense of engagement and motivation, creating a sustainable path towards improved self-management and enhanced quality of life. The process requires patience, self-compassion, and a commitment to consistent practice; but the rewards of improved focus, emotional regulation, and overall well-being are well worth the effort. Remember to celebrate small victories along the way and to seek support when needed. The path to managing ADHD is a journey best traveled with the support of others.

References

The Benefits of Mindfulness and Meditation for Mental Health and Well-Being – Factober. https://factober.com/article/the-benefits-of-mindfulness-and-meditation-for-mental-health-and-well-being-2/

Controlling Stress and anxiety through breathing exercises. | Cycle Against Suicide. https://www.cycleagainstsuicide.

com/2023/07/10/controlling-stress-and-anxiety-through-breathing-exercises/

Mastering the Waves: Powerful Emotional Regulation Tech.... https://www.coachingconsciousness.org/blog/mastering-the-waves-powerful-emotional-regulation-techniques-for-inner-harmony

flippy chain fidget toy review - Fidget Tech. https://fidget-tech.com/flippy-chain-fidget-toy/

Exploring Effective Therapies for Obsessive-Compulsive Disorder (OCD). https://mnclinicforhealth.com/exploring-effective-therapies-for-obsessive-compulsive-disorder-ocd/

The Transformative Power of Trauma-Focused CBT for Adults | Connections Wellness Group. https://connectionswellnessgroup.com/blog/the-transformative-power-of-trauma-focused-cbt-for-adults/

How to Stop Thinking About Work at 3am | Tips by Virtunus. https://tips.virtunus.com/tips/553ff2b8-bd04-4363-9ec1-facee93a1058/how-to-stop-thinking-about-work-at-3am

Conquering Exam Stress: Effective Strategies for Relief | Accela Marketing. https://www.accelamarketing.com/newsletter/conquering-exam-stress-effective-strategies-for-relief

How do you meditate for digestion?. https://kyaguide.com/wellness/how-do-you-meditate-for-digestion/

Preparing Mentally for Drug and Alcohol Rehab: Essential Steps - Seacrest Recovery Center Cincinnati Ohio. https://

seacrestrecoverycincinnati.com/preparing-mentally-for-drug-and-alcohol-rehab-essential-steps/

Complete Harmony Blog: Study: Exercise Can Help Treat Addiction. https://blog.completeharmonyrehab.com/2018/06/study-exercise-can-help-treat-addiction.html

19

Time Management and Organizational Strategies for Adults with ADHD

Building upon the foundation of mindfulness and meditation, we now turn to the practical application of time management and organizational strategies. These are crucial components in navigating the daily challenges posed by ADHD. While medication and mindfulness can significantly alleviate symptoms, effective strategies for managing time and organizing tasks are essential for translating these improvements into tangible changes in daily life. The key is to understand that these aren't "one-size-fits-all" solutions; rather, they represent a toolkit from which individuals can select and adapt methods best suited to their unique needs and preferences. The process is iterative, requiring experimentation, adjustment, and a degree of selfcompassion as you learn what works best.

One of the most pervasive challenges for adults with ADHD is the struggle with procrastination. This isn't simply laziness; it stems from a complex interplay of factors including difficulty initiating tasks, a tendency towards impulsivity, and a preference for immediate gratification over long-term goals. Overcoming procrastination requires a multi-pronged approach that addresses these underlying issues. Breaking down large tasks into smaller, more manageable steps can significantly reduce the feeling of being overwhelmed, making the task less daunting and more approachable. For example, instead of tackling a large writing project all at once, break it down into smaller, more achievable goals: outline the project, write one section per day, edit one section per day, and so on. This approach transforms an intimidating mountain into a series of manageable hills.

Time blocking is another invaluable technique. This involves scheduling specific blocks of time for particular tasks in your day. This provides a structured framework, minimizing the decision fatigue often experienced by individuals with ADHD. Instead of constantly deciding what to work on next, the schedule dictates the order, allowing you to focus on the task at hand without mental depletion. It's crucial to be realistic when creating a schedule, factoring in breaks and potential interruptions. Overly ambitious schedules can lead to frustration and a sense of failure, undermining the effectiveness of the strategy. Consider utilizing time-tracking apps to monitor your productivity and identify patterns of procrastination or time misallocation. This data can provide valuable insights into your working habits and inform adjustments to your schedule.

Externalizing your tasks is a powerful way to reduce mental clutter and improve task completion. This involves using external memory aids, such as to-do lists, calendars, and planning apps. Writing tasks down frees up valuable mental space, preventing crucial details from slipping through the cracks. These external aids should be easily accessible and visually clear. Experiment with different methods to find what works best for you, whether it's a traditional paper planner, a digital calendar, or a whiteboard. Color-coding tasks or using different visual cues can further enhance organization and prioritization. Consistency is crucial here; regularly updating your external memory aids ensures they remain effective tools.

Prioritization is an essential skill for effective time management. Learning to distinguish between urgent and important tasks is crucial. Using methods such as the Eisenhower Matrix (urgent/important matrix) can help to categorize tasks, enabling you to focus on the most critical items first. This approach helps to prevent getting bogged down in less important tasks, ensuring that your energy and time are directed towards activities that truly contribute to your goals. Delegating tasks where possible can also free up valuable time and mental energy, allowing you to focus on your strengths and areas of expertise.

Creating a supportive environment is crucial for successful implementation of these strategies. Minimize distractions by creating a dedicated workspace free from clutter and interruptions. Communicate your time management strategies to those around you, encouraging their understanding and support. This might involve setting boundaries around your work time, letting family members or colleagues know when you need uninterrupted focus. A supportive environment minimizes the likelihood of unexpected disruptions, allowing you to maintain concentration and progress efficiently.

The effective use of technology can be both a boon and a bane. While technology offers numerous productivity tools, it also presents opportunities for distraction. Mindfully selecting and utilizing productivity apps can enhance organizational skills. However, it is equally important to establish boundaries with technology, avoiding excessive scrolling or multitasking, which can hinder focus and productivity. Consider using website blockers or app timers to limit access to distracting platforms during work periods. The goal is to harness technology's positive aspects while mitigating its potential for distraction.

Regular review and adjustment are essential for optimizing your time management and organizational strategies. Periodically review your schedule, to-do lists, and productivity patterns to assess their effectiveness. Identify areas for improvement and adjust your approach accordingly. This ongoing evaluation ensures that your strategies remain relevant and effective in meeting your changing needs and priorities. Don't be afraid to experiment with different techniques and adapt your approach as needed. The goal is to find a system that works for you, not to adhere rigidly to a particular methodology.

Remember, the journey to improved time management and organization is a continuous process. There will be setbacks, moments of frustration, and challenges to overcome. Embrace these experiences as opportunities for learning and growth. Celebrate small victories and maintain a sense of self-compassion throughout the process. With consistent effort and the right strategies, you can significantly enhance your ability to manage time, organize tasks, and achieve your goals, leading to a more fulfilling and productive life.

Beyond specific techniques, consider the broader context of your lifestyle. Adequate sleep, regular exercise, and a balanced diet play a significant role in cognitive function and energy levels. Neglecting these foundational elements can undermine even the most meticulously planned organizational systems. Prioritizing self-care is not a luxury; it's a necessity for effective time management and overall well-being. This means actively scheduling time for activities that promote physical and mental health, such as exercise, hobbies, and social interaction.

Finally, remember that seeking professional support is not a sign of weakness but a sign of strength. A therapist specializing in ADHD can provide personalized guidance, helping you identify the specific challenges you face and develop tailored strategies to overcome them. They can also offer support and accountability, helping you stay motivated and on track. Cognitive Behavioral Therapy (CBT) is particularly effective in addressing the underlying cognitive distortions and maladaptive behaviors that contribute to time management difficulties in ADHD. Don't hesitate to utilize the expertise of professionals to enhance your journey towards effective self-management.

The path to effective time management and organization for adults with ADHD is not a linear progression, but rather a process of continuous refinement and adaptation. Through experimentation, perseverance, and a willingness to seek support, you can develop strategies that empower you to take control of your time, prioritize your tasks, and ultimately, enhance your overall quality of life. Remember to celebrate your successes along the way and approach any setbacks with self-compassion, recognizing that progress is not always smooth and consistent. By incorporating these strategies and maintaining a commitment to selfimprovement, you can unlock your full potential and live a more organized and fulfilling life.

References

Effective Time Management: Top 10 Tips to Boost Productivity. https://deepdecide.com/effective-time-management-tips/

5 Things I wish I knew before I started my new job - PEP WorldWide EU. https://pepworldwide.eu/5-things-i-wish-i-knew-before-i-started-my-new-job/

Leveraging A Virtual Assistants for Efficient Project Management - The First Pick VA Group. https://www.firstpickva.com/blog/leveraging-a-virtual-assistants-for-efficient-project-management

Inpatient Drug Rehab Programs in San Bernardino County: Helping Individuals Overcome Substance Abuse - SoCal Beach Recovery. https://socalbeachrecovery.com/inpatient-drug-rehab-programs-in-san-bernardino-county/

The Bucket of Life Skills: How One Hole Can Ruin the Whole Thing – Once In A Blue Moon. https://onceinabluemoon.ca/the-bucket-of-life-skills-how-one-hole-can-ruin-the-whole-thing/

How to Improve Focus and Efficiency | The Happy Mind. https://www.thehappymind.uk/blog/how-to-improve-focus-and-efficiency

Fuel Your Brain – Nootropics for Enhanced Cognitive Fuel Efficiency – Rosettas Tone Fine Art. https://rosettastonefineart.com/fuel-your-brain-nootropics-for-enhanced-cognitive-fuel-efficiency/

20

Support Groups and Social Connections for Individuals with ADHD

The journey to managing ADHD effectively isn't solely a personal one; it's profoundly intertwined with the support and understanding of others. While medication, mindfulness, and organizational techniques are crucial tools, the power of social connection and shared experience cannot be overstated. Feeling isolated and misunderstood is a common struggle for individuals with ADHD, and connecting with others who "get it" can be transformative. This isn't just about emotional support; it's about gaining practical insights, sharing strategies, and building a network that fosters resilience and mutual encouragement.

Support groups offer a safe and non-judgmental space to discuss the challenges of living with ADHD. These groups are not therapy sessions, but rather opportunities for peer-to peer learning and mutual support. You'll find yourself among individuals who understand the complexities of executive dysfunction, the frustrating experience of procrastination, and the emotional rollercoaster that can accompany ADHD. This shared understanding can significantly reduce feelings of isolation and self-blame. Instead of feeling like an anomaly, you'll discover you're part of a community facing similar obstacles and celebrating similar triumphs.

Within these supportive environments, you can gain valuable perspectives on coping mechanisms. What works for one person might not work for another, but hearing a variety of approaches—from time-blocking techniques to specific organizational apps—can broaden your own toolkit. Sharing your own successes and struggles provides an opportunity for reflection and refinement of your strategies. The simple act of articulating your challenges can provide clarity and identify areas for further improvement. The feedback from others within the group can offer fresh insights you may not have considered on your own.

Moreover, support groups cultivate a sense of belonging and validation. Hearing others describe experiences that mirror your own—from the hyperfocus that can lead to late-night work binges to the impulsivity that can derail well-laid plans —can be immensely validating. This shared experience counters the pervasive feeling of being "different" or "deficient," replacing it with a sense of normalcy and acceptance. It's empowering to realize you are not alone in your struggles.

Finding the right support group is crucial. Some groups may be more focused on specific aspects of ADHD, such as relationships, work, or parenting. Others might cater to particular demographics, such as adults, women, or individuals with co-occurring conditions. Researching and exploring different groups can help you find the best fit. Online support groups offer a broader reach and increased accessibility, allowing participation regardless of geographical location or scheduling constraints. However, in-person groups offer the unique benefit of face-to-face interaction and a stronger sense of community.

Beyond formal support groups, cultivating meaningful social connections can significantly enhance your overall wellbeing. Building relationships with friends, family, and colleagues who understand and support you is invaluable. Open communication with loved ones about your ADHD can help foster understanding and reduce misunderstandings. Explaining your challenges and needs clearly can prevent unnecessary conflict and improve relationships.

It's essential to carefully select the people you share your diagnosis with. Choose individuals who are likely to offer empathy and understanding rather than judgment or dismissal. It's completely valid to protect your emotional energy and to only confide in those who you trust will provide a safe and supportive environment. This selection process is vital in reducing the risk of additional stress and negative experiences. Remember that sharing your diagnosis is a personal choice, and it's perfectly acceptable to not share this information with everyone.

Building a social network isn't always easy. For many individuals with ADHD, social situations can be challenging. The social fatigue experienced by some can make maintaining friendships and social connections a significant effort. However, even small steps, such as attending a single meeting of a support group or reaching out to a friend or family member, can make a significant difference in your overall well-being.

In addition to support groups and close relationships, consider engaging in activities that foster social interaction and provide a sense of accomplishment. Joining a club, volunteering, or participating in a team sport can offer opportunities to connect with like-minded individuals and develop meaningful relationships. These activities offer a chance to focus on shared interests and develop a sense of belonging while simultaneously working on selfimprovement and developing new skills.

The benefits extend beyond simply combating loneliness and social isolation. Strong social connections have been shown to improve mental and physical health, boost resilience in the face of stress, and even contribute to improved treatment adherence. The support provided by others can reinforce positive behaviors and provide the encouragement needed to persevere through challenges. This social reinforcement can be particularly beneficial when facing setbacks in managing ADHD symptoms.

Remember, finding the right support system is a process. It may take time and experimentation to discover the social connections that best meet your needs. Don't be afraid to explore different options and find what feels right for you. Start with small steps, be patient with yourself, and celebrate your successes along the way. The journey towards effective ADHD management is significantly enhanced by building a strong support network that understands, accepts, and encourages you.

The development of robust social support structures should not be underestimated in the holistic management of ADHD. For instance, consider the specific challenges individuals with ADHD face in the workplace. Difficulties with time management, organization, and prioritization can lead to increased stress and decreased productivity. Having a supportive colleague or mentor who understands these challenges can make a significant difference. They can provide encouragement, offer practical advice, and help navigate workplace dynamics. This support network can help alleviate the feelings of inadequacy or failure that can be amplified in professional settings.

Furthermore, the social challenges extend beyond the workplace. Building and maintaining close relationships with friends and family can also be demanding. The impulsivity and emotional dysregulation often associated with ADHD can strain relationships. Open communication and a willingness to discuss the impact of ADHD on relationships are crucial. Seeking support from a therapist or counselor who specializes in ADHD can be beneficial in learning strategies for effective communication and conflict resolution. These therapeutic interventions can strengthen existing relationships and prevent the development of further social strain.

In addition to seeking professional assistance, exploring online communities and forums dedicated to ADHD can offer a valuable sense of community and shared understanding. These virtual spaces offer an accessible way to connect with others who share similar experiences and gain perspectives from individuals across diverse geographical locations. The anonymity offered by online platforms can make it easier for some individuals to share their struggles and vulnerabilities, leading to greater feelings of acceptance and self-compassion. However, it's important to be mindful of the potential downsides of online interaction, such as the potential for misinformation or negative experiences.

The significance of social support is not limited to adults. If you are a parent of a child with ADHD, creating a support network is equally essential. Support groups for parents of children with ADHD can provide invaluable advice, emotional support, and a shared understanding of the unique challenges involved in raising a child with ADHD. These groups can help reduce feelings of isolation and provide practical strategies for managing the various aspects of parenting a child with ADHD.

Remember, the effective management of ADHD requires a multifaceted approach that includes medication, therapy, and lifestyle modifications. But woven throughout this approach is the fundamental need for social connection and support. By actively seeking out support groups, cultivating meaningful relationships, and fostering a network of understanding individuals, you can significantly enhance your ability to manage your ADHD and live a more fulfilling and balanced life. This support system acts as a buffer against the challenges and provides encouragement and validation along the challenging journey of living with ADHD. It's a vital part of the holistic approach to managing this neurodevelopmental condition.

References

Recognizing Signs of Burnout and Strategies for Prevention. https://www.chattanoogacounselingandconsulting.com/post/recognizing-signs-of-burnout-and-strategies-for-prevention

Encouraging Funny Motivational Memes. https://www.oola.com/everyday-life/2559940/encouraging-memes/

Relax and Rejuvenate: Managing Stress for a Better Aging Experience – Reliv Affiliate. https://relivaffiliate.com/blogs/news/relax-and-rejuvenate-managing-stress-for-a-better-aging-experience

To Reduce Blood Pressure, Reduce Stress First – Talking About Men's Health. https://tamh.menshealthnetwork.org/to-reduce-blood-pressure-reduce-stress-first/

How Social Media Affects Mental Health Positively. https://etherapypoc.com/how-social-media-affects-mental-health-positively/

Personal Injury and Emotional Trauma: Seeking Therapy and Counseling Support. https://nyc-injury-attorneys.com/personal-injury-and-emotional-trauma-seeking-therapy-and-counseling-support/

Maintaining balance in life is crucial for overall well-being. https://www.brotherlevonxcommunityreporting.com/post/maintaining-balance-in-life-is-crucial-for-overall-well-being

21

ADHD and Anxiety Disorders

The intricate relationship between ADHD and anxiety disorders is a significant area of focus in adult ADHD treatment. The high comorbidity rate—meaning the frequent co-occurrence of both conditions in the same individual— highlights the importance of understanding their interplay and developing integrated treatment strategies. It's not simply a matter of one condition causing the other; rather, they often share underlying neurological vulnerabilities and overlapping symptoms, making accurate diagnosis and effective management crucial. A significant percentage of adults diagnosed with ADHD also meet the criteria for at least one anxiety disorder, such as generalized anxiety disorder (GAD), panic disorder, social anxiety disorder (SAD), or specific phobias. This co-occurrence presents both diagnostic and therapeutic challenges.

One of the primary diagnostic challenges stems from the symptom overlap. Both ADHD and anxiety disorders can manifest as restlessness, difficulty concentrating, irritability, and sleep disturbances. For instance, the hyperactivity and impulsivity often seen in ADHD can be misinterpreted as anxiety-driven behaviors, particularly in situations where an individual with ADHD struggles to manage their time or meet deadlines. Conversely, the worry and apprehension characteristic of anxiety disorders can be mistaken for inattentiveness or distractibility in ADHD. This overlap can lead to misdiagnosis or delayed diagnosis of either or both conditions, delaying appropriate intervention and ultimately impacting the individual's quality of life.

Furthermore, the shared underlying neurobiological mechanisms contribute to the high comorbidity rate.

Research suggests that dysfunction in specific brain regions, particularly those involved in executive function, emotional regulation, and the stress response system, are implicated in both ADHD and anxiety disorders. These shared vulnerabilities increase the likelihood of experiencing both conditions simultaneously. For example, individuals with ADHD may exhibit heightened sensitivity to stress and threat, making them more prone to developing anxiety. Similarly, the difficulty with emotional regulation commonly observed in ADHD can lead to increased anxiety in response to even minor stressors.

Effective diagnosis requires a thorough assessment that considers both conditions. Clinicians should utilize a comprehensive approach, employing standardized diagnostic interviews and rating scales for both ADHD and anxiety disorders. This may involve utilizing instruments like the Adult ADHD Self-Report Scale (ASRS) for ADHD and the Generalized Anxiety Disorder 7-item (GAD-7) scale or the Panic Disorder Severity Scale (PDSS) for anxiety disorders. Gathering collateral information from family members, partners, or colleagues can provide valuable insights into symptom presentation and the overall impact of both conditions on daily functioning. The diagnostic process must go beyond simply identifying symptoms; it necessitates a nuanced understanding of the individual's unique presentation, considering the temporal relationship between ADHD and anxiety symptoms and their respective severity.

Treatment for co-occurring ADHD and anxiety disorders necessitates an integrated approach, addressing both conditions concurrently. A purely symptom-focused approach often proves inadequate. Instead, a holistic strategy that combines pharmacological and non-pharmacological interventions is generally recommended. Medication can play a significant role in managing both ADHD and anxiety symptoms. Stimulant medications commonly used for ADHD, such as methylphenidate and amphetamine, can sometimes also reduce anxiety symptoms. However, it's important to carefully monitor for potential side effects, as stimulants can sometimes exacerbate anxiety in susceptible individuals. Non-stimulant medications, such as atomoxetine, can also be effective in managing both ADHD and anxiety. Furthermore, certain antidepressants, such as selective serotonin reuptake inhibitors (SSRIs) or serotoninnorepinephrine reuptake inhibitors (SNRIs), are frequently prescribed to manage anxiety and can sometimes be beneficial for ADHD-related symptoms like emotional dysregulation. The choice of medication should be tailored to the individual's specific symptom profile and response to treatment. Careful titration and monitoring are essential to ensure efficacy and minimize side effects.

Beyond medication, non-pharmacological interventions are crucial components of a comprehensive treatment plan.

Cognitive Behavioral Therapy (CBT) has emerged as an evidence-based treatment for both ADHD and anxiety disorders. CBT techniques can equip individuals with tools to manage their thoughts, feelings, and behaviors associated with both conditions. For example, CBT can help individuals identify and challenge anxiety-provoking thoughts, develop coping strategies for stressful situations, and improve emotional regulation skills. Similarly, CBT can help manage ADHD symptoms by addressing organizational challenges, improving time management, and enhancing impulse control. Mindfulness-based interventions, such as mindfulness meditation, have also demonstrated efficacy in reducing anxiety and improving attention and focus in individuals with ADHD. These interventions promote selfawareness, emotional regulation, and stress reduction, addressing crucial aspects of both conditions.

Lifestyle modifications can play a significant supportive role. Regular physical exercise, a balanced diet, adequate sleep hygiene, and stress reduction techniques are all essential elements of a holistic treatment plan. Establishing consistent routines and structuring daily activities can also enhance symptom management. Support groups can provide invaluable emotional support and a sense of community for individuals navigating these challenging conditions. The support of family and friends is also a vital factor in fostering a supportive environment that encourages adherence to treatment and promotes overall well-being.

The specific treatment plan should be individualized, considering the severity of both ADHD and anxiety symptoms, the individual's preferences, and their response to treatment. Regular monitoring of symptom improvement is essential to adjust treatment strategies as needed. Close collaboration between the individual, psychiatrist, psychologist, or other healthcare professionals involved in their care is crucial for optimal outcomes. Furthermore, ongoing research continues to illuminate the neurobiological underpinnings of these conditions and refine effective treatment approaches. This knowledge base evolves constantly, leading to improved diagnostic tools and treatment strategies.

In summary, the high comorbidity of ADHD and anxiety disorders necessitates a comprehensive approach that addresses both conditions simultaneously. Accurate diagnosis requires careful consideration of symptom overlap and a thorough evaluation employing appropriate diagnostic tools. Effective treatment hinges on an integrated strategy that combines pharmacological interventions tailored to the individual's needs, along with non-pharmacological approaches like CBT and mindfulness practices, coupled with essential lifestyle modifications and strong support systems. The ongoing collaboration between patient and healthcare professional is vital to monitor progress, make adjustments, and optimize treatment for sustained improvement in quality of life. This integrated approach offers the best chance for individuals to effectively manage both ADHD and anxiety, leading to improved functioning across various life domains. It's a complex issue, but with the right understanding and treatment, individuals can significantly improve their well-being and experience a better quality of life. The journey is not always easy, but with consistent effort and support, significant progress is achievable. Understanding the nuances of the interaction between these two conditions is a crucial step towards fostering successful management strategies. The future of treatment lies in personalized approaches that leverage the strengths of individual patients and optimize their care based on their unique needs. Furthermore, ongoing research will further illuminate this complex interaction and lead to even more effective interventions.

References

How much hydroxyzine to take for anxiety. https://hydroxyzine24h.top/how-much-hydroxyzine-to-take-for-anxiety/

Key Distinctions: Dual Diagnosis vs. Co-Occurring Disorders. https://harmonyjunctionrecovery.com/blog/difference-between-dual-diagnosis-and-co-occurring-disorders/

Chakhssi, F., Bernstein, D. P., & Ruiter, C. D. (2012). Early maladaptive schemas in relation to facets of psychopathy and institutional violence in offenders with personality disorders. Legal and Criminological Psychology. https://doi.org/10.1111/lcrp.12002

Ozempic: Revolutionizing Diabetes Management with a Once-Weekly Solution. https://1tamilmv.online/ozempic-the-ultimate-solution-for-weight-loss/

Finding the Best Harm OCD Therapist Near Me. https://ocdmantra.com/therapist/harm-ocd-therapist-near-me/

Coping Strategies for Bipolar Disorder | Solh Wellness. https://www.solhapp.com/blog/coping-strategies-for-bipolar-disorder

A Comprehensive List of Mental Illnesses. https://mapleavepub.com/a-comprehensive-list-of-mental-illnesses.html

The Synergy of Therapy and Medication: Enhancing Mental Health Treatment | Ellie Mental Health, PLLP. https://elliementalhealth.com/the-synergy-of-therapy-and-medication-enhancing-mental-health-treatment/

22

ADHD and Depression

The high comorbidity rate between ADHD and depression presents another significant challenge in adult ADHD treatment. Just as with anxiety, the co-occurrence isn't simply a matter of one condition causing the other; rather, it reflects a complex interplay of shared neurological vulnerabilities, overlapping symptoms, and potentially shared genetic predispositions. Understanding this intricate relationship is crucial for effective diagnosis and treatment. A substantial portion of adults diagnosed with ADHD also experience symptoms consistent with Major Depressive Disorder (MDD), persistent depressive disorder (dysthymia), or other depressive disorders. This overlap necessitates a careful diagnostic process to avoid misattribution of symptoms and ensure appropriate intervention.

The diagnostic process for co-occurring ADHD and depression requires a multi-faceted approach. Clinicians must rely not only on self-report measures, like the Adult ADHD Self-Report Scale (ASRS) or the Conners' Adult ADHD Rating Scales, but also incorporate collateral information from family members, partners, or close friends. These informants can offer valuable insights into the individual's behavior, mood, and overall functioning, particularly in areas where self-reported data might be less reliable due to symptom-related biases. Structured clinical interviews, such as the Diagnostic Interview for Genetic Studies (DIGS) or the Structured Clinical Interview for DSM-5 (SCID), are essential for a comprehensive assessment, meticulously differentiating between ADHD symptoms and those characteristic of depression. The challenge lies in disentangling symptoms that might appear similar, such as low motivation, fatigue, and difficulty concentrating, which can be present in both ADHD and depression. For example, while difficulty concentrating is a core feature of ADHD, in depression, it is often accompanied by feelings of hopelessness and worthlessness, which are not typical of ADHD inattentiveness. Similarly, while low motivation can be present in both conditions, the underlying emotional state differs significantly. In ADHD, it might manifest as procrastination or difficulty initiating tasks, whereas in depression, it is often rooted in a pervasive sense of lethargy and despair.

The overlapping symptoms create the primary diagnostic challenge, underscoring the need for a comprehensive clinical evaluation beyond simple checklists. Careful history taking, exploring the temporal sequence of symptom onset and their evolution over time, is essential. Did depressive symptoms precede or follow the onset of ADHD symptoms? Understanding this timeline can provide crucial insights into the causal relationships, if any, between the two conditions. Neuropsychological testing can also play a valuable role, helping to delineate cognitive deficits specifically associated with ADHD (e.g., working memory, executive function) from cognitive slowing or impairment related to depression. Further complicating the matter is the fact that some medications used to treat ADHD, particularly stimulants, can exacerbate existing depressive symptoms or even trigger new ones in susceptible individuals. Therefore, careful medication selection and close monitoring for side effects are paramount.

Once a diagnosis of both ADHD and depression is established, an integrated treatment plan must be developed. This approach recognizes the interconnectedness of the conditions and avoids treating them in isolation. The choice of treatment modalities will depend on several factors, including the severity of both conditions, the individual's preferences, and the presence of other co-occurring conditions. Pharmacological interventions often play a central role. For ADHD, stimulants like methylphenidate or amphetamine-based medications are frequently prescribed, although their use necessitates careful monitoring for potential depressive side effects. Non-stimulant medications, such as atomoxetine, can be an alternative, especially in individuals sensitive to stimulant-induced side effects. For depression, antidepressants, particularly selective serotonin reuptake inhibitors (SSRIs) or serotonin-norepinephrine reuptake inhibitors (SNRIs), are commonly used. The decision of which antidepressant to prescribe, and at what dosage, is made on a case-by-case basis, considering the individual's medical history, potential drug interactions, and response to previous treatments. In some cases, a combination of an ADHD medication and an antidepressant may be necessary, but this must be carefully managed due to potential drug interactions and the risk of side effects.

The careful titration of medications, starting with low doses and gradually increasing them as needed, is crucial to optimize efficacy and minimize adverse effects. Regular monitoring of medication effectiveness and side effects is essential to adjust the treatment regimen as needed.

Beyond pharmacological interventions, non-pharmacological approaches are equally vital. Psychotherapy, especially cognitive behavioral therapy (CBT), has proven highly effective in managing both ADHD and depression. CBT for ADHD helps individuals develop strategies for improving attention, organization, and emotional regulation. CBT for depression focuses on identifying and modifying negative thought patterns and behaviors that contribute to depressive symptoms. In the context of co-occurring ADHD and depression, a therapist might help the individual address both sets of symptoms simultaneously, creating a unified treatment plan. Mindfulness-based techniques, such as meditation and yoga, can also be beneficial in reducing stress, improving focus, and promoting emotional wellbeing. These techniques can complement pharmacological treatments, fostering a holistic approach to recovery.

Lifestyle modifications are an often-overlooked but crucial component of integrated treatment. Regular exercise, a healthy diet, sufficient sleep, and stress-reduction techniques, such as spending time in nature or engaging in hobbies, contribute significantly to mood stabilization and cognitive function. Establishing consistent routines can improve daily functioning by providing structure and predictability, which are particularly beneficial for individuals with ADHD. Social support is also critical. Connecting with supportive friends, family members, or support groups can provide a sense of belonging and reduce feelings of isolation, often prevalent in both ADHD and depression. Regular engagement with these support systems reinforces positive coping mechanisms and promotes adherence to treatment plans.

The treatment journey for co-occurring ADHD and depression requires patience and persistence. It's crucial for both the individual and the healthcare team to understand that setbacks are possible. The process involves ongoing monitoring, adjustments to treatment plans as needed, and open communication between the patient and their healthcare professionals. Regular review sessions are essential to track progress, modify medication dosages, and refine therapy strategies to optimize outcomes. The ultimate goal is to help individuals manage their symptoms, improve their quality of life, and enhance their overall functioning in various life domains, including work, social relationships, and personal well-being. The path to recovery may be long and challenging, but with a comprehensive, integrated treatment approach, meaningful improvements are attainable.

Furthermore, ongoing research continues to shed light on the underlying neurobiological mechanisms driving the comorbidity between ADHD and depression, paving the way for more targeted and effective interventions. Emerging research focuses on genetic susceptibility, brain imaging studies identifying neural correlates of symptom overlap, and investigating the role of neurotransmitters in the interplay of these conditions. This research holds immense promise for developing personalized treatment approaches that consider individual genetic profiles and neurobiological characteristics, allowing for a more precise and effective tailoring of therapeutic strategies. The collaborative effort between researchers, clinicians, and individuals with ADHD and depression will undoubtedly lead to more effective interventions and improved outcomes in the future. The development of digital tools and telehealth platforms also offers new avenues for providing more accessible and personalized treatment, especially for those with limited access to traditional healthcare settings. These advancements are crucial in fostering a more inclusive and effective approach to managing these conditions. In conclusion, addressing co-occurring ADHD and depression demands a comprehensive strategy, combining careful diagnostic assessment with an integrated treatment plan that encompasses pharmacological interventions, psychotherapy, lifestyle changes, and ongoing monitoring. This multipronged approach, combined with continued research, offers significant hope for individuals navigating the challenges posed by this complex comorbidity, promoting improved well-being and a better quality of life.

References

Effective Medications for Bipolar Disorder Treatment. https://mapleavepub.com/effective-medications-for-bipolar-disorder-treatment.html

Anxiety & Depression | Irwin & Associates. https://www.irwincoaching.ca/anxiety-depression

Why Someone Might Keep Bringing Up the Past - StartPoint Counselling. https://startpointcounselling.com.au/why-someone-might-keep-bringing-up-the-past/

Menopause | Alpha OBGYN. https://www.alphaobgyn.com/menopause/

Exploring the Connection Between Prescription Drug Rehab and Medication Management - The Nextep. https://thenextep.org/exploring-the-connection-between-prescription-drug-rehab-and-medication-management/

Assessment and Diagnosis of Stuttering. https://ndisspeechtherapy.com/assessment-and-diagnosis-of-stuttering

23

ADHD and Substance Use Disorders

The intricate relationship between attentiondeficit/ hyperactivity disorder (ADHD) and substance use disorders (SUDs) represents a significant clinical challenge. The co-occurrence of these conditions is far from coincidental; rather, it reflects a complex interplay of shared vulnerabilities, overlapping symptoms, and potentially shared genetic and environmental influences. Understanding this intricate relationship is crucial for effective diagnosis and treatment, leading to improved outcomes for individuals struggling with both conditions.

One critical aspect of this comorbidity lies in the shared neurobiological underpinnings. Both ADHD and SUDs involve dysfunction within the brain's reward circuitry, specifically impacting dopamine pathways. Dopamine, a neurotransmitter crucial for motivation, pleasure, and reward, plays a central role in both conditions. In ADHD, there's evidence suggesting a deficiency in dopamine function, leading to difficulties with attention, impulsivity, and hyperactivity. Individuals with ADHD may seek external stimuli, such as substances, to artificially boost dopamine levels and alleviate feelings of under-stimulation or boredom. Conversely, substance use itself dramatically alters dopamine levels, leading to reinforcement of substance-seeking behaviors. This overlap in neurobiological mechanisms provides a compelling explanation for the high rates of comorbidity.

Furthermore, the symptomatic overlap between ADHD and SUDs can complicate diagnosis. Impulsivity, a core symptom of ADHD, is also a significant risk factor for substance abuse. Individuals with ADHD may engage in impulsive behaviors, including substance use, without fully considering the consequences. Similarly, difficulties with executive function, such as planning and self-regulation, common in ADHD, can impair an individual's ability to control substance use, even when they recognize the potential negative impact. This shared symptomatology necessitates a thorough assessment, utilizing multiple sources of information including self-report measures, collateral information from family members or close friends, and behavioral observations, to differentiate between symptoms related to ADHD and those stemming from substance use.

Risk factors for the co-occurrence of ADHD and SUDs are multifaceted. Genetic predisposition plays a substantial role. Family history of both ADHD and substance abuse significantly increases the likelihood of developing both conditions. Environmental factors also contribute significantly. Exposure to trauma, chaotic family environments, and peer influence can all increase the risk of both ADHD and SUDs. Moreover, early onset of substance use, particularly before the age of 15, is strongly associated with a greater likelihood of developing comorbid ADHD. The earlier the substance use begins, the more likely it is to interfere with normal brain development and increase the vulnerability to both ADHD and subsequent substance dependence.

Diagnostic considerations for this comorbid presentation require a comprehensive and multifaceted approach. Clinicians must utilize standardized diagnostic tools to assess for both ADHD and specific SUDs. This often involves using rating scales specific to ADHD symptoms, such as the Adult ADHD Self-Report Scale (ASRS) and the Conners' Adult ADHD Rating Scales, in conjunction with structured clinical interviews for diagnosing substance use disorders, such as the DSM-5 criteria-based interviews, the SCID, or the MINI. It is critical to establish a clear temporal relationship between the onset of ADHD symptoms and the initiation of substance use. Determining which condition preceded the other can provide crucial insights into the nature of the comorbidity and inform treatment strategies. It is also vital to consider the possibility of other co-occurring disorders, such as depression or anxiety, which are frequently observed in individuals with both ADHD and SUDs. These conditions may exacerbate each other and complicate treatment.

Effective treatment for individuals with comorbid ADHD and SUDs requires an integrated and holistic approach, tailored to the individual's unique clinical presentation. This involves addressing both ADHD and SUDs simultaneously, rather than treating them sequentially. A common strategy utilizes a phased approach. The first phase often involves stabilizing the individual's substance use through detoxification and potentially medication-assisted treatment (MAT), such as methadone or buprenorphine for opioid dependence. Concurrently, or in a subsequent phase, ADHD symptoms are addressed using a combination of pharmacological and non-pharmacological interventions. Stimulant medications are often used for ADHD, but their use in individuals with SUDs requires careful monitoring due to the potential for abuse. Non-stimulant medications may be a safer alternative in some cases, but may prove less effective. The choice of medication needs to be made on a case by case basis.

Psychotherapy plays a crucial role in this integrated treatment plan. Cognitive behavioral therapy (CBT) is particularly effective in addressing both ADHD symptoms and substance use behaviors. CBT helps individuals identify and modify maladaptive thoughts and behaviors that contribute to substance use and difficulties with impulse control and emotional regulation. CBT can also teach coping strategies for managing cravings, stress, and other triggers for substance use. Other therapies, such as motivational interviewing and contingency management, can further enhance treatment effectiveness. Motivational interviewing assists individuals in recognizing the ambivalence surrounding their substance use and helps them move towards making positive changes. Contingency management uses positive reinforcement to encourage abstinence and adherence to treatment.

Family therapy can also be beneficial in supporting the individual and addressing family dynamics that may contribute to the development or maintenance of both conditions. Family involvement can be crucial in providing support, promoting accountability, and creating a positive environment for recovery. Support groups, such as those offered by organizations like Narcotics Anonymous or Alcoholics Anonymous, provide peer support and can improve recovery outcomes. Regular monitoring is critical, typically involving frequent clinical visits and drug screens to monitor treatment adherence and identify any potential relapses or complications.

Furthermore, addressing psychosocial factors such as housing instability, unemployment, or lack of social support is essential for sustained recovery. Connecting individuals with relevant community resources, such as job training programs, housing assistance, and social support networks, enhances their chances of successful long-term recovery. This integrated, multi-modal approach acknowledges the complexities of comorbid ADHD and SUDs, providing a more effective and comprehensive treatment strategy.

The prognosis for individuals with comorbid ADHD and SUDs is influenced by various factors, including the severity of each condition, the presence of other co-occurring disorders, the individual's level of motivation and engagement in treatment, and the availability and quality of support systems. Early intervention is crucial in improving outcomes, as early substance use can exacerbate ADHD symptoms and lead to more severe and chronic problems. While the challenges are significant, with a comprehensive and individualized treatment approach that combines medication, psychotherapy, and psychosocial support, many individuals can achieve significant improvements in their

ADHD symptoms and substance use patterns, leading to improved quality of life and sustained recovery.

Ongoing research continues to advance our understanding of the neurobiological mechanisms underlying the comorbidity between ADHD and SUDs, leading to the development of more targeted and effective treatments. Studies exploring the genetic basis of this comorbidity are identifying specific genes and pathways that may contribute to increased vulnerability. Neuroimaging techniques, such as fMRI and PET scans, are providing insights into brain function and structure in individuals with both conditions, revealing areas of dysfunction and guiding the development of more tailored interventions.

The future of treatment for this complex comorbidity promises to be increasingly personalized. This involves tailoring treatment approaches to individual characteristics, including genetic profiles, neurobiological features, and personal circumstances. Emerging technologies, such as digital therapeutics and telemedicine, offer opportunities for expanding access to evidence-based treatments, making them more convenient and accessible to individuals regardless of their geographical location or socioeconomic status.

In summary, the comorbidity of ADHD and SUDs presents a significant clinical challenge but one that is increasingly manageable with a comprehensive and individualized treatment strategy. By recognizing the complex interplay between these conditions, utilizing a multi-modal approach to treatment, and continuing to advance research in this area, we can significantly improve the lives of individuals facing this significant challenge, enabling them to live fulfilling and productive lives. The collaboration between healthcare providers, researchers, and individuals themselves will be crucial in achieving this goal. The future of treatment lies in personalized medicine, integrating advancements in neuroscience and technology to ensure that everyone receives the targeted and effective care they need to manage this difficult but treatable condition.

References

Adolescent Addiction Treatment. https://www.prescotthouse.com/blog/adolescent-addiction-treatment

How Do Opioids Affect the Brain? | Detox LA. https://detoxla.com/blog/how-do-opioids-affect-the-brain/

Best Rehabilitation Programs In La Puente, CA | Local Treatment. https://broadwaytreatmentcenter.com/blog/best-drug-rehabilitation-programs-in-la-puente-california-effective-and-personalized-addiction-treatment/

What Are the Most Effective Therapies for Teen Depression? - Alis Behavioral Health. https://www.alisbh.com/blog/what-are-the-most-effective-therapies-for-teen-depression

ADHD and Addiction: Breaking the Vicious Cycle. https://www.birchtreerecovery.com/blog/adhd-and-addiction

Breaking the Cycle: GLP-1 Agonists and Binge Eating Disorders – A Potential Therapeutic Approach – GLP-1 Wellness. https://glp1wellness.com/breaking-the-cycle-glp-1-agonists-and-binge-eating-disorders-a-potential-therapeutic-approach/

24

ADHD and Sleep Disorders

The close association between ADHD and sleep disturbances is a clinically significant observation, often overlooked in the initial assessment and treatment planning. While ADHD itself doesn't directly *cause* sleep problems, the core symptoms of inattention, hyperactivity, and impulsivity create a fertile ground for the development of various sleep disorders. The hyperactivity and difficulty regulating arousal, characteristic of ADHD, can manifest as insomnia, difficulty falling asleep, and frequent nighttime awakenings. Conversely, the inattentiveness and impulsivity can lead to poor sleep hygiene, irregular sleep schedules, and daytime sleepiness that further exacerbates ADHD symptoms. This creates a vicious cycle, where poor sleep worsens ADHD symptoms, leading to further sleep disruption.

The prevalence of sleep disorders in individuals with ADHD is considerably higher than in the general population. Studies consistently demonstrate a significantly increased risk of insomnia, narcolepsy, sleep apnea, and restless legs syndrome in adults with ADHD. This increased risk is not simply a matter of coincidence; several contributing factors intertwine to explain this complex relationship. Firstly, the neurobiological underpinnings of ADHD, involving imbalances in neurotransmitters like dopamine and norepinephrine, are also implicated in the regulation of sleep-wake cycles. These neurochemical imbalances can disrupt the natural circadian rhythm, making it difficult to fall asleep and stay asleep.

Secondly, the behavioral manifestations of ADHD, particularly hyperactivity and impulsivity, directly interfere with establishing and maintaining healthy sleep habits.

Individuals with ADHD may struggle with bedtime routines, finding it difficult to wind down and relax before sleep. They may engage in stimulating activities late into the evening, further delaying sleep onset. The impulsivity associated with ADHD can also lead to impulsive nighttime awakenings, disrupting sleep continuity. Poor sleep hygiene practices, such as inconsistent sleep schedules, exposure to bright light before bed, and excessive caffeine or alcohol consumption, are more common in this population, compounding the sleep problems.

Furthermore, the co-occurrence of other psychiatric comorbidities, frequently observed alongside ADHD, can further complicate sleep patterns. Anxiety and depression, frequently seen in individuals with ADHD, are themselves strongly linked to sleep disturbances. The worry and racing thoughts associated with anxiety can make it difficult to fall asleep and maintain sleep throughout the night. Similarly, the low mood and fatigue associated with depression contribute to increased sleepiness during the day and disrupted nighttime sleep. Therefore, addressing cooccurring conditions is paramount in effectively managing sleep problems in individuals with ADHD.

Diagnosing sleep disorders in individuals with ADHD can present unique challenges. The core symptoms of ADHD can often mimic the symptoms of certain sleep disorders, creating diagnostic ambiguity. For instance, daytime sleepiness, a common symptom of both ADHD and several sleep disorders, can be attributed to either condition, leading to diagnostic uncertainty. Therefore, a comprehensive assessment, including detailed sleep history, sleep diaries, polysomnography (a sleep study), and questionnaires to assess both ADHD and sleep disorders, is crucial for accurate diagnosis.

The treatment of sleep disorders in adults with ADHD requires a multi-faceted approach, integrating pharmacological and non-pharmacological interventions. In cases of insomnia, cognitive behavioral therapy for insomnia (CBT-I) is often the first-line treatment. CBT-I focuses on identifying and modifying maladaptive thoughts and behaviors that contribute to insomnia, teaching individuals skills to improve sleep hygiene, and establishing consistent sleep routines. This approach has proven highly effective in improving sleep quality and reducing insomnia symptoms. It is important to note that the efficacy of CBT-I is enhanced when delivered by trained professionals specializing in insomnia and ADHD. Relapse prevention is also a key element of the treatment.

Pharmacological interventions may be necessary in cases where CBT-I alone is insufficient. However, the choice of medication requires careful consideration, taking into account potential interactions with ADHD medications. Some commonly used sleep medications, such as benzodiazepines, can exacerbate ADHD symptoms or interact negatively with stimulant medications. Therefore, a careful evaluation of the individual's medication profile is necessary before initiating any sleep medication. Nonbenzodiazepine hypnotics, like zolpidem or eszopiclone, may be considered as safer alternatives, but their use should be short-term and carefully monitored due to potential side effects and risks of dependence.

In addition to addressing specific sleep disorders, improving overall sleep hygiene is crucial for individuals with ADHD. This involves implementing strategies to promote better sleep habits, such as establishing a regular sleep-wake schedule, creating a relaxing bedtime routine, optimizing the sleep environment (dark, quiet, cool), and limiting exposure to electronic devices before bed. Regular exercise, a balanced diet, and stress management techniques, such as mindfulness or yoga, can also contribute to improved sleep quality.

The management of restless legs syndrome (RLS), frequently co-occurring with ADHD, involves both pharmacological and non-pharmacological approaches. Dopamine agonists, such as pramipexole or ropinirole, are often prescribed to alleviate RLS symptoms. However, these medications can potentially interact with ADHD medications, highlighting the need for close collaboration between the prescribing psychiatrist and other healthcare professionals involved in the patient's care. Nonpharmacological strategies include regular exercise, avoiding caffeine and alcohol, and applying heat or cold compresses to the legs.

Sleep apnea, characterized by repeated pauses in breathing during sleep, requires specialized treatment, typically involving continuous positive airway pressure (CPAP) therapy. This therapy involves wearing a mask that delivers pressurized air to keep the airways open during sleep. The use of CPAP can significantly improve sleep quality and overall health in individuals with sleep apnea. In some cases, surgery may be necessary to address underlying anatomical issues contributing to sleep apnea. It's crucial for patients with suspected sleep apnea to undergo a thorough sleep study to confirm the diagnosis and determine the appropriate treatment strategy.

Addressing sleep disorders in adults with ADHD is a crucial aspect of comprehensive care. The complex interplay between ADHD and sleep requires a multidisciplinary approach, involving collaboration between psychiatrists, sleep specialists, and other healthcare professionals. By integrating effective assessment, personalized treatment plans that combine pharmacological and nonpharmacological strategies, and a focus on sleep hygiene, we can significantly improve the sleep quality and overall wellbeing of individuals with ADHD. It is essential to remember that treating sleep problems is not merely about resolving a comorbidity; it's about improving the overall functioning and quality of life for individuals living with ADHD, breaking the vicious cycle between poor sleep and impaired attention, hyperactivity, and impulsivity. The long-term implications of untreated sleep disorders are significant, impacting cognitive function, mood, and overall health, therefore prioritizing comprehensive sleep management is vital for successful ADHD treatment.

Finally, ongoing monitoring and adjustments to treatment strategies are necessary to optimize outcomes and address the evolving needs of the individual.

References

Drug And Alcohol Rehab Tamworth | Addiction Advocates. https://www.addictionadvocates.com/locations/drug-and-alcohol-rehab-tamworth/

Yi-Lei, P., & Hsiang-Yuan, L. (2020). Comparative Efficacy of Methylphenidate and Atomoxetine on Social Adjustment in Youths with Attention-Deficit/Hyperactivity Disorder. Journal of Child and Adolescent Psychopharmacology, 30(3), 148-158.

Unlocking the Relationship Between ADHD and Sleep. https://www.nightowlpsychotherapy.com/post/understanding-the-complex-relationship-between-adhd-and-sleep

Prevalence of sleep disorder diagnoses and sleep medication prescriptions in individuals with ADHD across the lifespan: a Swedish nationwide register-based study | BMJ Mental Health. https://mentalhealth.bmj.com/content/26/1/e300809?rss=1

Are Sleep Disorders Genetic? - Acibadem Health Point - ACIBADEM Hospitals - Acibadem Health Group. https://www.acibademhealthpoint.com/are-sleep-disorders-genetic/

Embracing the New Luxury of Being Offline and Unplugged | SoulFire Adventures. https://soulfireadventures.com/embracing-the-luxury-of-being-offline/

What Causes Sleep Disorders? | Buy Sleeping Tablets And Pills Online. https://www.simplysleepingpills.com/what-causes-sleep-disorders/

What food should I not eat at night? | Green Garden. https://www.greengarden.com.bd/blog/green-garden-blogs-1/what-food-should-i-not-eat-at-night-6

Movsessian, T. (2022). Association Between Therapeutic Interventions and Quality of Life in People with Autism. https://core.ac.uk/download/580005469.pdf

What Keeps You Awake At Night?. For a year or so, after my retirement… | by Jude Manickam | Medium. https://judemanickam.medium.com/what-keeps-you-awake-at-night-4f5e6906c6da?source=user_profile---------6------------------------

Restless Legs Syndrome Symptoms At Night Little Beauty Blog. https://littlebeautyblog.com/health-wellness/restless-legs-syndrome-symptoms-at-night/

Sleep Your Way to a Healthier Heart | Comanche County Memorial Hospital Blog. http://blog.ccmhhealth.com/sleep-your-way-to-a-healthier-heart/

Anti-Snoring Mouth Guard Shows Promise For Many People. https://www.wafb.com/story/4547612/anti-snoring-mouth-guard-shows-promise-for-many-people/

The Role of Mouth Guards in Treating Sleep Apnea. https://www.dentexdental.com.au/the-role-of-mouth-guards-in-treating-sleep-apnea/

Discover the Benefits of Rem Therapy for PTSD. https://mapleavepub.com/revolutionizing-ptsd-treatment-with-rem-therapy.html

25

ADHD and Borderline Personality Disorder

Differentiating between Adult ADHD (Attention-Deficit/Hyperactivity Disorder) and EUPD (Emotionally Unstable Personality Disorder, also known as Borderline Personality Disorder) can be challenging due to overlapping symptoms, such as impulsivity, emotional dysregulation, and difficulty maintaining relationships. However, the underlying causes, core features, and treatment approaches for these conditions are distinct. Below is a breakdown to help differentiate between the two:

---

1. Core Features

Adult ADHD:

- Inattention: Difficulty sustaining focus, forgetfulness, disorganization, and trouble completing tasks.

- Hyperactivity/Restlessness: Inner restlessness, fidgeting, or excessive talking (though hyperactivity may be less pronounced in adults).

- Impulsivity: Acting without thinking, interrupting others, or making hasty decisions.

- Executive Dysfunction: Poor time management, difficulty planning, and procrastination.

- Emotional Dysregulation: Mood swings, irritability, and frustration, often linked to unmet needs or sensory overload.

EUPD (Borderline Personality Disorder):

- Emotional Instability: Intense, rapidly shifting emotions (e.g., anger, sadness, anxiety) that are often disproportionate to the situation.

- Fear of Abandonment: Extreme efforts to avoid real or perceived abandonment, leading to unstable relationships.

- Identity Disturbance: Unstable self-image or sense of self.

- Impulsivity: Self-damaging behaviors (e.g., substance abuse, reckless spending, self-harm, or suicidal behavior).

- Chronic Feelings of Emptiness: A persistent sense of inner void or boredom.

- Stress-Related Paranoia or Dissociation: Temporary paranoid thoughts or dissociation under stress.

---

2. Key Differences

Primary Focus:

- In Adult ADHD, the primary difficulty lies with attention, focus, and executive functioning.

- In EUPD, the core issue is emotional instability, fear of abandonment, and identity disturbance.

Emotional Dysregulation:

- In Adult ADHD, mood swings are often reactive (e.g., frustration due to unmet needs or sensory overload).

- In EUPD, mood swings are intense, rapid, and often unrelated to external triggers.

Impulsivity:

- In Adult ADHD, impulsivity is more about acting without thinking (e.g., interrupting others or making hasty decisions).

- In EUPD, impulsivity often manifests as self-destructive behaviors (e.g., self-harm, substance abuse, or reckless spending).

Relationships:

- In Adult ADHD, struggles with relationships are often due to forgetfulness, inattentiveness, or difficulty following through on commitments.

- In EUPD, relationship struggles stem from fear of abandonment, intense emotional reactions, and a pattern of unstable interpersonal dynamics.

Self-Image:

- In Adult ADHD, self-esteem issues may arise from chronic underachievement or criticism related to forgetfulness or disorganization.

- In EUPD, there is often an unstable self-image, with individuals shifting between extremes of self-worth.

Triggers:

- In Adult ADHD, symptoms are often triggered by tasks requiring sustained attention or executive functioning.

- In EUPD, symptoms are often triggered by interpersonal conflicts or perceived rejection.

Chronic Feelings:

- In Adult ADHD, individuals may feel frustrated, overwhelmed, or bored due to executive dysfunction.

- In EUPD, individuals often experience chronic feelings of emptiness, worthlessness, or fear of abandonment.

---

3. Onset and Course

- Adult ADHD: Symptoms typically begin in childhood (before age 12) but may go undiagnosed until adulthood. Symptoms are chronic but can improve with treatment.

- EUPD: Symptoms usually emerge in late adolescence or early adulthood. The course can be variable, with some individuals experiencing improvement over time, especially with therapy.

---

4. Comorbidity

- Adult ADHD: Often co-occurs with anxiety, depression, or substance use disorders.

- EUPD: Frequently co-occurs with mood disorders (e.g., depression, bipolar disorder), PTSD, or eating disorders.

---

5. Diagnostic Tools

- Adult ADHD: Diagnosed using clinical interviews, rating scales (e.g., ADHD Rating Scale), and sometimes neuropsychological testing. A history of childhood symptoms is essential.

- EUPD: Diagnosed using clinical interviews and structured tools like the Structured Clinical Interview for DSM-5 (SCID-5) or the Borderline Personality Disorder Severity Index (BPDSI).

---

6. Treatment Approaches

Adult ADHD:

- Medication: Stimulants (e.g., methylphenidate, amphetamines) or non-stimulants (e.g., atomoxetine).

- Therapy: Cognitive Behavioral Therapy (CBT), coaching, or skills training for executive functioning.

- Lifestyle Adjustments: Organizational tools, routines, and environmental modifications.

EUPD:

- Therapy: Dialectical Behavior Therapy (DBT) is the gold standard. Other options include Mentalization-Based Therapy (MBT) or Transference-Focused Psychotherapy (TFP).

- Medication: No specific medication for EUPD, but medications may be used to manage co-occurring symptoms (e.g., mood stabilizers, antidepressants).

- Self-Help: Emotional regulation skills, mindfulness, and distress tolerance techniques.

---

7. Key Questions to Differentiate

- For ADHD:

- Do symptoms of inattention, hyperactivity, or impulsivity date back to childhood?

- Are the emotional reactions tied to frustration with tasks or unmet needs?

- Is there a family history of ADHD?

- For EUPD:

- Are the emotional reactions intense and disproportionate to the situation?

- Is there a pattern of unstable relationships and fear of abandonment?

- Are there self-destructive behaviors or chronic feelings of emptiness?

---

8. When Both Conditions Coexist

It's possible for someone to have both ADHD and EUPD, which can complicate diagnosis and treatment. In such cases, a thorough assessment by a mental health professional is crucial to address both conditions effectively.

Conclusion

While both conditions share some overlapping symptoms, the core features, triggers, and treatment approaches differ significantly. A detailed clinical evaluation, including a thorough history and use of diagnostic tools, is essential to differentiate between the two and provide appropriate care. If you suspect either condition, consult a mental health professional for an accurate diagnosis and tailored treatment plan.

26

Emerging Pharmacological Treatments for ADHD

The landscape of pharmacological treatments for ADHD is constantly evolving, with ongoing research yielding promising new avenues for improving symptom management and enhancing the lives of adults affected by this condition. While stimulant and non-stimulant medications remain cornerstones of current treatment, several emerging pharmacological approaches hold significant potential.

One area of intense investigation is the development of novel stimulant formulations. Traditional extended-release formulations aim for consistent medication levels throughout the day, but individual responses vary significantly. Newer approaches focus on personalized delivery systems, potentially adjusting release profiles based on real-time monitoring of physiological markers or even user input. This could lead to significantly improved efficacy and a reduction in unwanted side effects by tailoring medication delivery to individual needs and daily rhythms. For example, research is exploring implantable drug delivery systems that could provide a continuous and stable supply of medication, reducing the need for daily oral administration. While still in early stages of development, the potential benefits of such systems in managing ADHD symptoms are considerable, potentially alleviating the burden of daily pill-taking and ensuring consistent therapeutic levels.

Beyond enhanced stimulant delivery, researchers are actively investigating new drug targets. A deeper understanding of the neurobiological mechanisms underlying ADHD has identified potential pathways beyond those currently addressed by existing medications. This has opened doors to explore novel compounds acting on different neurotransmitter systems or focusing on specific aspects of ADHD symptomatology. For instance, research is ongoing into the potential role of certain neuropeptides and their receptors in ADHD pathophysiology. These neuropeptides, which modulate neuronal communication in distinct ways compared to dopamine and norepinephrine, are being explored as potential drug targets for developing new medications with unique mechanisms of action and potentially reduced side effect profiles. Preclinical studies utilizing animal models of ADHD have revealed promising results, but further human trials are crucial to establish efficacy and safety in individuals with ADHD.

Another exciting area is the exploration of non-stimulant medications with novel mechanisms. Atomoxetine, currently a common non-stimulant option, targets norepinephrine reuptake. However, research is expanding to explore other neurotransmitter systems, including serotonin and glutamate, which play significant roles in attention, impulse control, and emotional regulation. Drugs targeting these systems could offer alternative treatment options for individuals who do not respond well to stimulants or experience intolerable side effects. Furthermore, research into the role of inflammation in ADHD has sparked interest in developing anti-inflammatory medications as potential adjunctive therapies. Chronic inflammation has been implicated in several neurological and psychiatric conditions, and some preliminary studies suggest a possible link to ADHD. While not directly targeting ADHD's core neurotransmitter imbalances, anti-inflammatory medications could potentially alleviate some associated symptoms and improve overall treatment outcomes in conjunction with standard ADHD medications. Further research is essential to evaluate the effectiveness and long-term implications of such approaches.

The development of combination therapies is also a significant trend. Given the multifaceted nature of ADHD, utilizing a combination of pharmacological and nonpharmacological approaches often yields the most successful outcomes. However, research is also exploring the potential benefits of combining different medications. For instance, combining a stimulant medication with a non-stimulant medication or with a medication targeting a different neurotransmitter system might lead to synergistic effects, improving symptom control while minimizing individual side effects. This strategy is particularly pertinent for individuals experiencing incomplete symptom remission with monotherapy. Careful clinical trials are necessary to identify optimal medication combinations and determine their efficacy and safety profile for varying ADHD symptom profiles and comorbidities.

Furthermore, advancements in our understanding of genetics and epigenetics are paving the way for personalized medicine in ADHD treatment. Genetic testing can identify individual variations in genes related to medication metabolism and response, allowing for more precise medication selection and dosage adjustments. This can improve treatment effectiveness and minimize side effects by tailoring the approach to the individual's unique genetic makeup. This personalized approach could significantly impact the future of ADHD treatment, moving away from a "one-size-fits-all" model towards highly individualized interventions that maximize therapeutic benefits while minimizing risks. Larger-scale studies are needed to fully understand the interplay between genetics, epigenetics, and treatment response, enabling the development of truly personalized treatment algorithms.

Despite significant advancements, numerous challenges remain. Many currently investigated medications are still in early clinical trial phases, and their long-term safety and efficacy require further evaluation. Moreover, understanding the complex interplay of genetics, environment, and individual experiences in shaping ADHD presentation remains an area of ongoing research. The lack of robust biomarkers for ADHD also presents a challenge. Objective measures to confirm diagnosis and monitor treatment response are crucial to streamlining the diagnostic process and evaluating therapeutic interventions effectively. Continued research into neuroimaging techniques and other biological markers holds promise in this area.

The development of new digital therapeutics offers exciting possibilities. Technology-based interventions, such as mobile apps providing cognitive training, behavioral feedback, and personalized medication reminders, have shown promise in improving ADHD management. These digital tools can be readily integrated into existing treatment plans and offer personalized support for individuals, supplementing traditional approaches. Moreover, the integration of telemedicine into ADHD care has expanded access to specialist services, especially in rural or underserved areas. However, rigorous evaluation of these interventions' longterm efficacy and their integration into existing healthcare systems remains critical. The development of standardized protocols for assessing the effectiveness of digital therapeutics is also crucial.

Finally, understanding the specific neurobiological mechanisms underlying the co-occurrence of ADHD with other mental health conditions, like anxiety and depression, is paramount. This knowledge will help in designing more effective treatments targeting both the core symptoms of ADHD and comorbid conditions. A holistic approach, integrating medication management, psychotherapy, lifestyle interventions, and digital therapeutics, tailored to the individual's unique profile, will likely be the most effective approach in the future. This necessitates continued multidisciplinary collaboration between psychiatrists, neurologists, psychologists, and other healthcare professionals.

In conclusion, the future of pharmacological treatments for ADHD holds immense promise. The development of novel medications, personalized medicine approaches, and the integration of digital therapeutics are reshaping the landscape of ADHD treatment, offering potential for more effective and individualized interventions. However, ongoing

research, rigorous clinical trials, and a concerted multidisciplinary effort are essential to fully realize the potential of these advancements and translate them into improved outcomes for adults with ADHD.

References

Liang, X., Yeh, C. H., Domínguez D., J. F., Poudel, G., Swinnen, S. P., & Caeyenberghs, K. (2021). Longtidunial fixed-based analysis reveals rstoration of white matter-alterations following balance training in young brain injured patients. https://doi.org/10.1016/j.nicl.2021.102621

The Best Medicine for ADD: A Comprehensive Guide to Finding the Right Treatment - The Cognitive Orbit. https://www.sdpuo.com/what-is-the-best-medicine-for-add/

How Does ADHD Correlate With Other Mental Health Conditions? | TMS Health and Wellness. https://www.tmshealthandwellness.com/how-does-adhd-correlate-with-other-mental-health-conditions/

27

Advances in Non Pharmacological Interventions

The remarkable progress in pharmacological interventions for Adult ADHD, as detailed in the previous chapter, should not overshadow the equally significant advancements occurring in non-pharmacological approaches. These methods, often used in conjunction with medication or as standalone treatments, offer a multifaceted strategy for managing ADHD symptoms and improving overall wellbeing. This section explores the burgeoning field of nonpharmacological interventions, focusing on digital therapeutics and neurofeedback, two rapidly developing areas with substantial promise.

Digital interventions represent a paradigm shift in ADHD treatment delivery. The ubiquitous nature of smartphones and readily accessible internet connectivity has opened up unprecedented opportunities for providing accessible, affordable, and personalized support. These interventions encompass a wide range of applications, from mobile apps designed to track symptoms and manage medication adherence to sophisticated cognitive training programs aimed at improving attention, working memory, and executive functions.

One of the most promising aspects of digital interventions is their ability to personalize treatment.

Traditional therapeutic approaches often involve a "one-size-fits-all" model, where interventions are tailored to general symptom profiles. However, the heterogeneity of ADHD symptoms means that a more individualized approach is often necessary. Digital platforms can leverage data collected from users to tailor interventions to their specific needs and responses, dynamically adjusting the intensity and type of intervention based on ongoing assessment. For example, a person struggling with time management might receive tailored prompts and reminders via a mobile app, while someone experiencing difficulty with emotional regulation might be directed to specific mindfulness exercises or cognitive behavioral therapy (CBT) modules.

The use of gamification techniques has further enhanced the engagement and efficacy of digital interventions. By integrating game mechanics like points, rewards, and challenges, these apps can motivate users to actively participate in their treatment and track their progress. This is especially beneficial for individuals with ADHD who may struggle with motivation and sustained effort. The competitive and rewarding aspects of gamified interventions can foster a sense of accomplishment and encourage consistent engagement, ultimately leading to improved adherence and better outcomes. Numerous apps are currently available, each offering a unique combination of features and functionalities. However, critical evaluation of their evidence base is crucial, as the quality and efficacy of these apps vary significantly. Rigorous clinical trials are essential to validate the effectiveness of these interventions and establish clear clinical guidelines for their implementation.

Beyond simple symptom tracking and medication reminders, digital interventions are incorporating more sophisticated therapeutic techniques. For instance, many apps incorporate elements of CBT, providing users with tools and strategies for managing their symptoms and improving their coping skills. These CBT modules can be delivered in a highly personalized and accessible manner, overcoming some of the limitations associated with traditional face-to-face therapy, such as cost, accessibility, and scheduling challenges. Moreover, some apps utilize artificial intelligence (AI) to provide personalized feedback and support, adapting to the individual's needs and progress in real-time. This personalized feedback loop can significantly enhance the effectiveness of the intervention and improve engagement.

However, the integration of AI and digital technologies raises important ethical considerations. Data privacy and security are paramount, and rigorous protocols are necessary to ensure the responsible use of personal data collected through these platforms. Transparency in the algorithms used and clear communication with users about data handling practices are essential to build trust and promote responsible innovation. Furthermore, the potential for bias in algorithms needs careful consideration, ensuring that digital interventions are equitable and accessible to all populations.

Neurofeedback, a technique that involves monitoring brainwave activity in real-time and providing feedback to the individual, offers another promising avenue for nonpharmacological ADHD treatment. The premise of neurofeedback lies in the ability to train individuals to regulate their brainwave patterns, thereby improving attention, focus, and impulse control. This is achieved through sensors placed on the scalp, which measure brainwave activity. The individual receives feedback through visual or auditory cues, indicating when their brainwave patterns are within a desired range. Through repeated practice, individuals learn to self-regulate their brainwave activity, leading to improved cognitive function and reduced ADHD symptoms.

Various neurofeedback protocols are employed, with each targeting specific brainwave frequencies associated with different cognitive processes. For instance, some protocols focus on enhancing attention by increasing the activity of certain brainwave frequencies, while others address impulsivity by reducing the activity of other frequencies.

The efficacy of neurofeedback has been a subject of ongoing debate and research. While some studies have shown promising results, others have yielded less conclusive findings. The heterogeneity of ADHD symptoms, coupled with variations in neurofeedback protocols and methodologies, has made it challenging to establish definitive conclusions regarding its effectiveness. However, recent meta-analyses suggest that neurofeedback can be a beneficial adjunct to other ADHD treatments, especially when combined with other therapeutic approaches.

The integration of neurofeedback with other nonpharmacological interventions, such as mindfulness training and CBT, holds particular promise. Mindfulness training techniques, such as meditation and deep breathing, can complement neurofeedback by enhancing self-awareness and promoting emotional regulation. CBT can provide individuals with the cognitive skills and coping strategies necessary to apply the self-regulation skills learned through neurofeedback to real-life situations. This integrated approach may enhance the long-term effectiveness of neurofeedback by providing individuals with a broader range of tools and strategies for managing their ADHD symptoms.

Furthermore, the development of new technologies and techniques in neurofeedback is continuously improving its accessibility and efficacy. For example, the use of portable and user-friendly neurofeedback devices is making it more convenient for individuals to engage in home-based treatment. The incorporation of virtual reality (VR) technology offers immersive and engaging training environments, enhancing motivation and engagement during neurofeedback sessions. However, the high cost of neurofeedback, coupled with the need for specialized training for practitioners, remains a significant barrier to wider access.

In conclusion, the field of non-pharmacological interventions for Adult ADHD is rapidly expanding, offering a wide range of options for individuals seeking to manage their symptoms and improve their quality of life. Digital interventions, with their personalized and accessible nature, are revolutionizing treatment delivery, while neurofeedback provides a promising avenue for training self-regulation skills. However, ongoing research, rigorous clinical trials, and careful consideration of ethical implications are essential to fully realize the potential of these advancements and ensure their responsible implementation. The future of ADHD treatment lies in a multi-faceted approach that integrates pharmacological and non-pharmacological interventions, tailored to the unique needs and preferences of each individual. A truly holistic approach encompassing medication, therapy, lifestyle modifications, and technological advancements provides the best chance for lasting improvements in the lives of adults with ADHD. The integration of these various approaches – combining the power of medication with the personalized support of digital tools and the brain-training potential of neurofeedback – signifies a paradigm shift towards a more comprehensive and effective approach to adult ADHD management. This integrated strategy promises not only symptom relief but also a path towards greater self-awareness, self-management, and improved overall well-being. The future is bright, but continued research and responsible development are crucial to ensuring equitable access and optimal outcomes for all.

References

Unlocking Potential: Exploring the Power of ABA Therapy. – Hour Power has what it takes.. https://hourpower.biz/unlocking-potential-exploring-the-power-of-aba-therapy-2/

How To Focus and Enhance Productivity with Mistikist. https://mistikist.com/how-to-focus-and-enhance-productivity-with-mistikist/

Benefits of Neurofeedback Therapy for Depression. https://neurolaunch.com/neurofeedback-therapy-depression/

ADHD Tools To Resist Substance Abuse - Launch Centers. https://launchcenters.com/adhd-tools-for-substance-abuse/

Sabbella, S. R., Kaszuba, S., Leotta, F., & Nardi, D. (2023). Gesture Recognition for Human-Robot Interaction Through Virtual Characters. Lecture Notes in Computer Science. https://doi.org/10.1007/978-981-99-8718-4_14

28

Personalized Medicine and Treatment Optimization in ADHD

The integration of pharmacological and nonpharmacological interventions, as discussed previously, represents a crucial step towards more effective ADHD management. However, the future of ADHD treatment lies not just in the combination of these approaches, but in their *personalization* . The "one-size-fits-all" approach to treatment is rapidly becoming obsolete, replaced by a paradigm shift toward personalized medicine. This personalized approach recognizes the inherent heterogeneity of ADHD, acknowledging that individuals experience the disorder differently and respond variably to interventions. This section explores the exciting advancements in personalized medicine and treatment optimization for adult ADHD.

The foundation of personalized medicine lies in a deeper understanding of the individual. This encompasses a comprehensive assessment extending beyond standard diagnostic criteria. It includes a detailed exploration of an individual's unique symptom profile, encompassing not only the core symptoms of inattention, hyperactivity, and impulsivity, but also co-occurring conditions such as anxiety, depression, sleep disorders, and substance use disorders. These co-occurring conditions significantly influence treatment decisions and outcomes. For example, an individual with ADHD and comorbid anxiety may require a different medication regimen compared to someone with ADHD alone, potentially necessitating a careful balancing act between managing ADHD symptoms and minimizing the risk of exacerbating anxiety. Similarly, an individual's preexisting medical conditions, such as cardiovascular disease or epilepsy, may necessitate adjustments to medication selection and dosage.

Beyond the clinical presentation, personalized medicine incorporates genetic testing. While not currently a standard practice in all ADHD clinics, pharmacogenomics is gaining traction. Pharmacogenomics examines how an individual's genetic makeup influences their response to specific medications. By analyzing specific genes, clinicians can predict the likelihood of a positive response to a particular medication, as well as potential side effects. This predictive capability allows for more informed treatment decisions, minimizing trial-and-error approaches and potential adverse effects. For example, certain genetic variations have been linked to a higher risk of adverse effects from stimulant medications, such as increased heart rate or blood pressure. Identifying these variations beforehand allows clinicians to select alternative medications or adjust dosages accordingly, optimizing treatment efficacy and safety. Furthermore, ongoing research is exploring the role of other genetic markers in understanding the pathophysiology of ADHD and identifying potential therapeutic targets for novel treatments.

Beyond genetics, personalized medicine considers lifestyle factors. This holistic approach recognizes the interplay between an individual's physical and mental health, highlighting the importance of addressing lifestyle factors such as diet, exercise, sleep hygiene, and stress management. Regular exercise, for instance, has been shown to have a positive impact on ADHD symptoms, improving focus, attention, and executive function. A healthy diet, rich in fruits, vegetables, and omega-3 fatty acids, can also contribute to better cognitive function and mood regulation. Conversely, poor sleep hygiene and chronic stress can significantly exacerbate ADHD symptoms. Integrating lifestyle interventions into the treatment plan, alongside medication and therapy, represents a crucial aspect of personalized medicine. This requires a collaborative approach between the individual, their clinician, and potentially other healthcare professionals such as dietitians or sleep specialists.

The use of digital technologies also plays a critical role in personalized medicine for ADHD. Digital therapeutics, such as mobile apps and online platforms, offer personalized interventions tailored to the individual's specific needs and preferences. These apps can provide real-time feedback, track symptom patterns, and deliver customized interventions, such as cognitive behavioral therapy (CBT) modules, mindfulness exercises, or medication reminders. The personalized nature of these interventions allows for greater engagement and adherence to treatment, improving overall outcomes. Data collected through these apps can also provide valuable insights into treatment response and potential areas for optimization.

This data-driven approach allows clinicians to make more informed adjustments to the treatment plan, ensuring it remains effective and personalized throughout the course of care.

Furthermore, the use of wearable technology, such as smartwatches and fitness trackers, can provide objective data on activity levels, sleep patterns, and heart rate variability, which can be helpful in assessing treatment response and identifying potential triggers for symptom exacerbation. The integration of this data into the treatment plan allows for a more holistic and comprehensive understanding of the individual's experience with ADHD, enhancing the precision and effectiveness of personalized interventions. The future likely holds even more sophisticated applications of digital technologies, such as artificial intelligence (AI) driven tools that can analyze large datasets to predict treatment response and identify optimal treatment strategies for specific individuals.

Another crucial element of personalized medicine is the patient's active participation in their treatment. The concept of shared decision-making emphasizes the importance of collaborative communication between the clinician and the individual with ADHD. This involves discussing treatment options, weighing the potential benefits and risks, and collaboratively establishing treatment goals. This collaborative approach empowers the individual to take ownership of their treatment plan, fostering greater engagement and adherence. Regular feedback sessions provide opportunities to assess treatment response, adjust the plan as needed, and address any challenges that may arise. The patient's feedback, alongside objective data from digital tools and genetic testing, paints a comprehensive picture, enhancing the effectiveness of personalized interventions.

However, the widespread adoption of personalized medicine in ADHD treatment faces challenges. The cost of genetic testing and digital therapeutics can be a barrier for some individuals. Moreover, there is a need for increased research to further refine and validate personalized treatment approaches. Further research is needed to identify and characterize the specific genetic and environmental factors that contribute to the heterogeneity of ADHD and to develop more targeted and effective interventions. This includes larger, well-designed clinical trials that evaluate the efficacy and safety of various personalized treatment strategies, as well as the development of robust outcome measures that capture the complexities of ADHD and its impact on daily life. Additionally, there's a need for more training and education for healthcare professionals to adequately implement personalized medicine approaches. Clinicians need to be equipped with the knowledge and skills to interpret genetic test results, utilize digital technologies effectively, and facilitate shared decision-making with their patients.

In conclusion, personalized medicine represents a significant advancement in the treatment of adult ADHD. By integrating genetic information, lifestyle factors, digital technologies, and shared decision-making, clinicians can tailor interventions to meet the unique needs of each individual, maximizing treatment efficacy and minimizing adverse effects. While challenges remain in terms of cost, research, and implementation, the move toward personalized medicine holds immense promise for transforming the landscape of ADHD treatment, paving the way for a future where individuals with ADHD can achieve optimal well-being and lead fulfilling lives. The ongoing development and refinement of personalized medicine strategies will continue to improve the lives of those affected by ADHD, ultimately leading to more effective, targeted, and sustainable outcomes. The integration of cutting-edge technology with a deep understanding of individual needs is not merely a future aspiration but the driving force shaping the current evolution of ADHD treatment.

References

Holistic Addiction Treatment Near Columbia, MO. https://aviaryrecoverycenter.com/rehab-near-columbia-mo/

How Neuroscience Research is Improving Mental Health Treatments. https://research-studies-press.co.uk/2024/07/05/how-neuroscience-research-is-improving-mental-health-treatments/

What Is Holistic Medicine & How Will It Change The World? - MALIBU MAMA LOVES. https://malibumamaloves.com/what-is-holistic-medicine-how-will-it-change-the-world/

ðâï¸ The Sun's Radiant Influence on Our Mood and ADHD âï¸ð. https://www.lifefitbrainfit.com/post/the-sun-s-radiant-influence-on-our-mood-and-adhd

Digital mental health platforms: Revolutionizing Access to Mental Health Support – Health education. http://healltheducation.info/digital-mental-health-platforms/

China's education sector becomes smarter with digital technologies - Xinhua Silk Road. https://en.imsilkroad.com/p/333332.html

Personalized Approach to Holistic Health | Finland Region. https://finlandregion.com/23709-personalized-approach-to-holistic-health-20/

Autism And Parkinson's: Is There A Connection? | Above and Beyond Therapy. https://www.abtaba.com/blog/autism-and-parkinsons

29

Ongoing Research and Unanswered Questions in Adult ADHD

Despite significant advancements in understanding and treating adult ADHD, numerous unanswered questions remain, highlighting the need for ongoing research. A key area requiring further investigation is the precise neurobiological underpinnings of the disorder. While we know that ADHD involves dysfunction in several brain regions, including the prefrontal cortex, striatum, and cerebellum, the exact mechanisms driving these deficits are still unclear. Research employing advanced neuroimaging techniques, such as functional magnetic resonance imaging (fMRI) and diffusion tensor imaging (DTI), is crucial in identifying specific neural pathways and networks implicated in ADHD symptom expression. Moreover, longitudinal studies tracking brain development in individuals with ADHD from childhood into adulthood are essential to understand the trajectory of neurobiological changes and their relationship to symptom presentation and treatment response. This longitudinal perspective is crucial as ADHD symptoms can evolve over time, and understanding these developmental trajectories is vital for tailoring effective interventions.

Another significant gap in our knowledge concerns the complex interplay between genetic and environmental factors in the etiology of ADHD. While twin and family studies have consistently demonstrated a strong heritable component, identifying specific genes responsible for increasing ADHD risk remains a challenge. Genome-wide association studies (GWAS) have identified several candidate genes, but these findings often lack replication across different studies and populations. Furthermore, the influence of environmental factors, such as prenatal exposure to toxins, perinatal complications, and early childhood experiences, on ADHD risk and symptom severity is not fully understood. Epigenetic studies, which investigate how environmental factors can modify gene expression without altering the underlying DNA sequence, offer promising avenues for unraveling the complex interplay between genes and environment in ADHD. These studies are crucial to developing preventative strategies and personalized interventions targeting specific vulnerabilities.

The heterogeneity of ADHD symptoms presents a considerable challenge for research and treatment. Individuals with ADHD exhibit a wide range of symptom profiles, with some primarily exhibiting inattention, others predominantly hyperactivity-impulsivity, and many experiencing a combination of both. This variability makes it difficult to develop universally effective treatments. Further research is needed to identify subtypes of ADHD based on distinct neurobiological mechanisms, cognitive profiles, and response to different interventions. The development of more refined diagnostic tools, including sophisticated neuropsychological assessments and biomarkers, is crucial for identifying these subtypes and ensuring appropriate treatment matching. This involves investigating the heterogeneity not only in symptom presentation but also in the co-occurrence of other psychiatric disorders, such as anxiety, depression, and substance use disorders, which often complicate the diagnosis and treatment of ADHD.

Current treatment approaches for adult ADHD primarily focus on pharmacological interventions and behavioral therapies. While stimulant medications are often effective in reducing core ADHD symptoms, a significant proportion of individuals do not achieve full remission or experience intolerable side effects. Research exploring alternative pharmacological treatments, such as non-stimulant medications and other novel compounds, is urgently needed. Moreover, the optimal combination of pharmacological and non-pharmacological interventions remains a subject of ongoing investigation. For instance, the effectiveness of different types of behavioral therapies, such as cognitive behavioral therapy (CBT) and mindfulness-based interventions, needs further study to determine their optimal delivery methods and their interaction with medication. The long-term effectiveness and sustainability of various interventions also need investigation; many studies focus on short-term outcomes, but understanding the long-term effects is crucial for developing comprehensive and enduring treatment plans.

The impact of ADHD on various aspects of adult life, such as relationships, work performance, and overall quality of life, requires further investigation. Studies examining the social, occupational, and emotional consequences of ADHD are essential for developing comprehensive support services and interventions. Research needs to focus on understanding the specific challenges faced by adults with ADHD in different life domains and developing targeted interventions to address these challenges effectively. This could include developing workplace accommodations, social skills training programs, and relationship counseling tailored to the unique needs of individuals with ADHD. The assessment of functional outcomes should not just rely on self-report; objective measures of work performance, relationship satisfaction, and quality of life, complemented by the perspective of family members or colleagues, are critical for a holistic understanding.

Furthermore, there is a need for more research on the longterm effects of ADHD and its treatments. While many studies focus on short-term outcomes, understanding the long-term impact of ADHD and the potential consequences of long-term medication use is crucial. This requires longitudinal studies tracking individuals with ADHD across many years, assessing not only the persistence of symptoms but also their impact on various life outcomes. This comprehensive tracking is essential for addressing potential concerns related to medication use over extended periods and for informing the development of long-term management strategies that promote both efficacy and patient well-being.

The development and implementation of personalized medicine approaches for ADHD represent a significant frontier in research. This involves identifying biomarkers that predict treatment response and tailoring interventions to individual needs. Research exploring genetic, neurobiological, and clinical characteristics that could inform personalized treatment strategies is crucial. This personalized approach promises to improve treatment efficacy and minimize adverse effects, leading to more effective and sustainable outcomes. Integrating genetic testing, neuroimaging data, and comprehensive clinical assessments to personalize treatment plans is an active area of investigation, with the promise of significantly improving the lives of individuals with ADHD. However, ethical considerations related to genetic testing and data privacy need careful consideration alongside the research endeavors.

Finally, research into effective strategies for improving medication adherence is essential. Many individuals with ADHD struggle with medication adherence, potentially compromising treatment effectiveness. Studies exploring different approaches to enhancing medication adherence, such as motivational interviewing, education programs, and technology-based support, are needed to improve outcomes. This focus requires considering not only the clinical efficacy of medication but also the factors that influence a patient's adherence and ability to engage in treatment. Addressing this issue will be crucial to improving long-term outcomes for individuals with ADHD.

In conclusion, while considerable progress has been made in understanding and treating adult ADHD, numerous unanswered questions remain. Further research is crucial to unraveling the complex neurobiological mechanisms underlying the disorder, identifying subtypes of ADHD, developing more effective treatments, understanding the long-term impact of ADHD and its treatments, implementing personalized medicine approaches, and improving medication adherence. By addressing these areas, we can move towards a future where individuals with ADHD can lead fulfilling lives with optimal well-being. The ongoing research efforts, focusing on both the biological underpinnings and the lived experiences of adults with ADHD, are not simply academic exercises; they are critical to improving the lives of millions who grapple with the daily challenges this condition presents. The collaborative efforts of researchers, clinicians, and individuals with ADHD are fundamental to building a future of better understanding, diagnosis, and treatment for this prevalent condition.

References

Uhrig, S. (2016). The involvement of central L-type calcium channel subtypes CaV1.2 and CaV1.3 in alcohol dependence and comorbid mental disorders. https://doi.org/10.11588/heidok.00021487

Hypnotherapy: The Science Behind It (and its impact on the brain). https://physiofitpt.com/the-science-behind-hypnotherapy-and-its-impact-on-the-brain/

Elkhaled, W., Selmi, O., & Dandan, A. (2023). Shared delusion amidst COVID-19 pandemic in 23-year-old monozygotic twins. Psychiatry Research. https://doi.org/10.1016/j.psycr.2023.100145

Genetics and Athletic Potential Nature vs Nurture. https://dashsports.org/2024/07/15/genetics-and-athletic-potential-nature-vs-nurture/

Li, H., Zhao, Q., Huang, F., Cao, Q., Qian, Q., Johnstone, S. J., Wang, Y., Wang, C., & Sun, L. (2017). Increased Beta Activity Links to Impaired Emotional Control in ADHD Adults With High IQ. Journal of Attention Disorders. https://doi.org/10.1177/1087054717739120

Setting Goals for PTSD Recovery Success | HealthyPlace. https://aws.healthyplace.com/blogs/traumaptsdblog/2017/11/goal-setting-during-ptsd-recovery

Exploring the Potential of Microdosing and Psychedelics for Bipolar Depression - Tetrahydrocannabinol. https://tetrahydrocannabinol.com/microdosing-and-psychedelics-for-bipolar/

Yan, M., Shi, Y., Su, C., He, J., Li, J., Wu, N., Ye, S., Shi, Y., Zhou, C., Li, Z., Ding, X., Wang, R., & Feng, Y. (2023). Cognitive behavioral therapy combined with head and face tuina/massage for negative emotions and sleep disorders in patients with protracted withdrawal symptoms: A study protocol for a randomized controlled trial. Research Square (Research Square). https://doi.org/10.21203/rs.3.rs-2790059/v1

Unveiling the Future: Trends in Personalized Medicine Research – OHE MATERIALS. https://ohematerials.org/personalized-medicine-research/

ADHD Revolution: Psychiatry's Role in Transforming Lives | Dr. Ryan Sondergard. https://drryansondergard.com/psychiatry-adhd/adhd-revolution-psychiatrys-role-in-transforming-lives/

30

Resources and Support for Adults with ADHD and Their Families

The journey of understanding and managing adult ADHD is rarely a solitary one. For individuals diagnosed with ADHD, their families, and the healthcare professionals supporting them, access to a robust network of resources and support is paramount. This section explores the diverse landscape of available resources, aiming to empower individuals and families to navigate the challenges of ADHD effectively.

Firstly, let's consider the resources specifically designed for adults with ADHD. These resources can range from self-help books and online communities to professional therapeutic interventions. Numerous self-help books offer practical strategies for managing symptoms like time management, organization, and emotional regulation. These books often provide worksheets, checklists, and exercises to aid in the implementation of these strategies. Many are written by clinicians with extensive experience treating ADHD, offering a balanced perspective informed by both research and clinical practice. However, it's crucial to remember that while self-help resources can be incredibly valuable, they should not replace professional guidance. They are best used as a supplementary tool to complement professional treatment.

Online communities dedicated to ADHD offer a unique space for connection and support. Forums, social media groups, and online support networks provide a platform for individuals to share their experiences, exchange coping strategies, and find empathy from others who understand the challenges they face. This shared experience can be incredibly validating and empowering. However, caution should be exercised in relying solely on online information. While these communities can offer valuable insights and support, the information shared may not always be accurate or evidence-based. It is essential to critically evaluate the information obtained and to supplement it with information from reliable sources.

Professional therapeutic interventions are a cornerstone of effective ADHD management. Cognitive Behavioral Therapy (CBT) is a widely used evidence-based approach that helps individuals identify and modify unhelpful thinking patterns and behaviors contributing to ADHD-related difficulties. CBT for ADHD may involve strategies to improve attention, organization, planning, and emotional regulation. Another effective approach is coaching, which can provide personalized support and guidance in developing effective strategies for managing daily tasks and achieving personal goals. Coaches often work collaboratively with individuals to develop individualized plans, setting realistic goals and providing ongoing support and accountability.

For individuals struggling with specific symptoms, specialized therapies may be beneficial. For example, individuals with significant difficulties with emotional regulation may benefit from Dialectical Behavior

Therapy (DBT). DBT teaches skills in mindfulness, distress tolerance, emotion regulation, and interpersonal effectiveness, which can be incredibly helpful in managing the emotional challenges associated with ADHD. Furthermore, occupational therapy can help individuals develop strategies to improve their organizational skills and daily functioning. This might involve assistive technology, environmental modifications, or strategies for managing sensory sensitivities, which can be common among individuals with ADHD.

Moving beyond individual resources, the support network extends to include family members and loved ones. The impact of ADHD often extends beyond the individual, affecting family dynamics, relationships, and overall family well-being. Family therapy can provide a valuable avenue for understanding the challenges presented by ADHD, improving communication patterns, and developing strategies for supporting the individual with ADHD while preserving family harmony. Support groups specifically designed for family members of individuals with ADHD offer a space to share experiences, learn effective coping strategies, and find emotional support from others in similar situations. These groups can be particularly helpful in normalizing the challenges and fostering a sense of community.

Educational resources are also crucial, both for individuals with ADHD and their families. Understanding the nature of ADHD, its symptoms, and its impact on daily life can significantly improve the ability to manage the condition effectively. Websites of reputable organizations, such as CHADD (Children and Adults with AttentionDeficit/Hyperactivity Disorder), offer detailed information about ADHD, its diagnosis, and its treatment. Furthermore, educational materials tailored for families can help educate children and adolescents about ADHD and foster empathy and understanding within the family unit.

The role of healthcare professionals extends beyond the initial diagnosis and treatment. Ongoing support and monitoring are crucial for optimizing treatment effectiveness and managing any potential side effects. Regular check-ups with psychiatrists or other healthcare providers specializing in ADHD management are essential to ensure that medication is appropriately adjusted and that other interventions are effective. Collaboration between healthcare providers is also important to ensure holistic care. For example, collaboration between psychiatrists, therapists, and occupational therapists can offer a comprehensive and tailored approach to managing ADHD symptoms.

Further resources exist to address the financial implications of living with ADHD. Depending on the individual's circumstances and location, support might be available through government programs or non-profit organizations dedicated to assisting individuals with disabilities. Navigating the paperwork and application processes for these programs can be challenging, and seeking assistance from social workers or advocacy groups specializing in disability services can be invaluable.

Finally, advocacy organizations play a crucial role in supporting individuals with ADHD and their families.

These organizations often provide resources, information, and support to those affected by ADHD. They may advocate for policies that benefit individuals with ADHD, raise awareness about the condition, and fund research into ADHD. Connecting with such organizations can provide a sense of belonging, support, and empowerment. They often offer opportunities to connect with others, access information and resources, and participate in advocacy efforts.

In conclusion, a comprehensive support system is critical for managing the multifaceted challenges of adult ADHD. The resources available are diverse and extensive, encompassing self-help tools, professional therapies, family support, educational materials, healthcare professionals, financial assistance programs, and advocacy organizations. By accessing and utilizing the appropriate resources, individuals with ADHD, their families, and their support network can navigate the condition's complexities and create a path towards a fulfilling and productive life. The key is to

actively seek out these resources and build a support system tailored to individual needs and circumstances.

Understanding the options available, knowing where to find them, and proactively engaging with them are essential steps towards effective management and a better quality of life. The journey may have its challenges, but with the right support, it is a journey that can be navigated successfully. The future of adult ADHD management lies not only in further research but also in the effective utilization of the existing resources and the continued development of even more comprehensive and accessible support systems.

References

Unleashing the Power Within: Female Empowerment | Health Centre NZ. https://healthcentre.nz/unleashing-the-power-within-female-empowerment/

Empowering Strategies for Anxiety Group Therapy. https://neurolaunch.com/anxiety-group-therapy-activities/

What is Cognitive Behavioral Therapy. https://www.christiancounselingcertification.com/post/what-is-cognitive-behavioral-therapy

Tips and Techniques for Families Seeking Addiction Assistance – Sober Mart. https://sobermart.com/tips-and-techniques-for-families-seeking-addiction-assistance/

Acknowledgments

This book would not have been possible without the support and contributions of many individuals.

First and foremost, I extend my deepest gratitude to the individuals with ADHD who shared their personal experiences and insights. Their courage and openness provided invaluable perspectives that shaped the content and tone of this work, helping to create a compassionate and informative resource.

I am also profoundly grateful to the healthcare professionals—psychiatrists, neurologists, psychologists, and clinicians—who generously offered their expertise and guidance. Their clinical insights and critical reviews greatly enhanced the accuracy and relevance of this book.

A special thank you to my incredible team for their unwavering support and belief in this project. The editorial team's dedication and professionalism were instrumental in bringing this book to life. I am particularly indebted to Dr. Rajesh Nair for his insightful guidance and meticulous attention to detail.

My heartfelt thanks to Dr. Nismen Lathif for contributing the foreword and to Dr. Smitha C.A. for her thoughtful suggestions.

Finally, I owe immense gratitude to my family and friends for their patience, understanding, and encouragement throughout the demanding writing process. Their love and support were essential to completing this work.

Appendix

This appendix points to some essential supplemental resource materials to enhance the reader's understanding of Adult ADHD.

List of Resources: Please search in the internet for following.

ASRS: Adult ADHD Self-Report Scale which is essential tool reporting to clinicians .

CAARS: Conners' Adult ADHD Rating Scales .This is for use by clinicians to reach a diagnosis of Adult ADHD.

I would like to add a Summary of NICE (National Institute of Clinical Excellence) Guidelines for Management of Adult ADHD here.

Treatment Principles

- Multimodal Approach:

Combine

pharmacological,

psychological, and lifestyle interventions.

- Shared Decision-Making:

Tailor treatment to

patient preferences,

risks, and functional goals.

- Stepped Care:

- Mild impairment: Start with psychoeducation and psychological therapies.

- Moderate-severe impairment: Offer medication alongside psychological support.

---

3. Pharmacological Treatment

First-Line Medications

- Stimulants:

- Methylphenidate (oral or long-acting): First-choice for most adults.

- Lisdexamfetamine: If methylphenidate is ineffective or poorly tolerated.

- Monitoring:

- Baseline cardiovascular assessment (BP, heart rate, ECG if risk factors).

- Regular reviews for efficacy, side effects (e.g., appetite loss, insomnia), and misuse risk.

Second-Line/Alternatives

- Non-Stimulants:

- Atomoxetine: For patients at risk of stimulant misuse or with comorbid anxiety.

- Guanfacine (off-label): Consider if stimulants and atomoxetine are unsuitable.

- Antidepressants (e.g., bupropion): Not routinely recommended but may help comorbid depression.

---

4. Psychological Interventions

- Cognitive Behavioral Therapy (CBT):

- Focus on organizational skills, emotional regulation, and coping strategies.

- ADHD Coaching: Practical support for time management, planning, and goal-setting.

- Group Therapy: Peer support and skill-building in structured settings.

---

5. Special Populations

- Pregnancy/Breastfeeding:

- Avoid stimulants unless benefits outweigh risks; consider non-stimulants (e.g., atomoxetine) or psychological therapies.

- Substance Use Disorders:

- Prioritize non-stimulants (atomoxetine) or specialist-managed stimulant use.

- Comorbid Mental Health Conditions:

- Treat the most impairing condition first (e.g., severe depression) or integrate ADHD treatment with comorbid care.

---

6. Monitoring and Safety

- Regular Follow-Up:

- Assess medication adherence, side effects, and functional improvement (e.g., work, relationships).

- Cardiovascular Monitoring: Annual checks for patients on stimulants.

- Misuse Risk: Screen for diversion or non-prescribed use, particularly in high-risk individuals.

---

7. Non-Recommended Interventions

- Antipsychotics: Avoid unless for comorbid psychosis.

- Routine Benzodiazepines: Not recommended for core ADHD symptoms.

- Dietary Supplements (e.g., omega-3): Insufficient evidence for standalone use.

---

8. Key Takeaways

- Early Intervention: Reduces long-term impairment in education, employment, and relationships.

- Holistic Care: Address physical health (e.g., sleep, diet) and social needs (e.g., workplace adjustments).

- Cultural Sensitivity: Consider stigma, accessibility, and patient beliefs in care planning.

Summary: NICE guidelines prioritize stimulant medications (methylphenidate or lisdexamfetamine) as first-line for moderate-severe adult ADHD, combined with CBT and lifestyle strategies. Atomoxetine is key for high-risk populations. Regular monitoring, patient involvement, and comorbidity management are essential. Always refer to the latest NICE guidelines (NG[X]) for full details.

Glossary

This glossary defines some other key terms used throughout the book related to Adult ADHD:

CBT: Cognitive Behavioral Therapy

DSM-5: Diagnostic and Statistical Manual of Mental Disorders, 5th Edition

And finally

DIVA-5: What is DIVA-5?

DIVA-5 is a Diagnostic Interview for ADHD in adults, available in many languages worldwide.

The DIVA Foundation aims to lower the threshold for proper diagnostic assessment of ADHD in adults worldwide, with the help of many colleagues and at the lowest possible costs. **DIVA-5** is the successor to DIVA 2.0, the semi-structured Diagnostic Interview for Adult ADHD, and is based on the criteria for ADHD in DSM-5.

DIVA-5 asks about the presence of ADHD symptoms in adulthood as well as childhood, the chronicity of these symptoms, and significant lifetime impairments due to these symptoms.

DIVA-5 has been adjusted for children, age 5-17 (Young DIVA-5) and for people with Intellectual Disability (DIVA-5 ID).

DIVA was first developed in Dutch. As the need for a readily available, semi-structured, diagnostic instrument for research and clinical assessment became apparent, translations into other languages were requested. These translations have been completed and the number of available languages is growing monthly. Professionals in psychiatry worldwide have increasing access to the interview.

Executive Functions: Cognitive processes such as planning, organizing, working memory, and inhibitory control. **Inattention:** Difficulty sustaining focus and attention. **Impulsivity:** Acting on urges without thinking through the consequences.

Hyperactivity: Excessive physical activity and restlessness. **Comorbidity:** The presence of one or more additional disorders or conditions alongside ADHD.

Author Biography

Dr Shafy Kalakkattil Muthalif, FRCPsych{UK) is a Consultant Psychiatrist in the United Kingdom with more than twenty years of experience specializing in diagnosing and treating Adult ADHD. He is currently working with Essex Partnership University Trust. He is passionate about providing compassionate and evidence-based care to individuals with ADHD and is committed to advancing the understanding and treatment of this condition. He is a Fellow of the Royal College of Psychiatrists and has received many positive feedbacks from Patients and Colleagues for treating ADHD patients successfully.